TEETH

OTHER BOOKS BY MICHAEL R. JACKSON AVAILABLE FROM TCG

A Strange Loop

TEETH

A Coming-of-Rage Musical Comedy

BOOK AND LYRICS BY **Michael R. Jackson**

BOOK AND MUSIC BY **Anna K. Jacobs**

Based on the film Teeth *by Mitchell Lichtenstein*

THEATRE COMMUNICATIONS GROUP / NEW YORK / 2025

Teeth is published by Theatre Communications Group, Inc.,
520 Eighth Avenue, 20th Floor, Suite 2000, New York, NY 10018-4156

TCG books are exclusively distributed to the book trade by Consortium Book Sales and Distribution.

Library of Congress Control Number: 2025026447 (paperback and ebook)
ISBN 978-1-63670-245-2 (paperback) / ISBN 978-1-63670-246-9 (ebook)
A catalog record for this book is available from the Library of Congress.

www.tcg.org
Follow us on Instagram @tcg_gram

Book design and composition by Lisa Govan
Cover art and design by Anabelle Plaza

First Edition, December 2025

To our teacher, William Finn

"I think The Good Book is missing some pages."

—FROM "ICICLE" BY TORI AMOS

CONTENTS

FOREWORD

Mitchell Lichtenstein

About twenty years ago, when I finished my script for a movie called *Teeth*, I sent it to my manager to see if he could help me get it produced. After reading it, he advised me never to show the script to anyone else, that anyone who read this script would not want to work with me—ever. And then he ghosted me.

I ran up against similar resistance as I shopped the script around myself, but because I believed in its message—and in its humor—I eventually decided to produce it completely independently. And even as we began production, the unusual opposition to the subject matter continued. When we started the casting process, we found that many actors' agencies refused to submit their clients for consideration. (Despite this, I can't imagine a better group of actors than those who eagerly came aboard, and I will always be grateful for their work and for the trust they put in me.)

Another hurdle went up when, with some trepidation, we went to Texas to scout locations. We were relieved by the warm welcome given to us by the Film Commission's representative, and on that first day of scouting, he showed us some very promising key locations: homes, schools, and hospitals. But the next morning, on what was to be our second day of scouting, he didn't show up. Nor did he answer our calls. It turns out he hadn't read the script until the previous night, and now that he had, he was busy calling all the locations he had shown us and advising them against allowing us to film there because our movie was pornography.

This is all to say that even years later, and with the movie having gained cult status, had anyone proposed adapting this story for the stage—and as a musical!—I'd have called them deranged. But then, I hadn't yet met Anna K. Jacobs and Michael R. Jackson.

The impetus for the movie was the *vagina dentata* myth itself, which I learned about in a college class taught by the dynamic and inspiring Camille Paglia. It's an ancient and pervasive myth with many variations, but it typically involves a female (sometimes a female animal) whose genitalia conceal penectomizing teeth, which the hero, a male (again, sometimes an animal), must conquer to restore societal order (i.e., male dominance). The myth is referenced time and again in popular culture, though disparately and indirectly: the Greek myth of the Medusa who turns men to stone, rigid but impotent; the beguiling but noxious yonic orchids in late nineteenth-century decadent literature; and the Alien Queen in the film *Aliens*, with her lubricious hidden teeth. All have been described as expressions of *vagina dentata*.

Why, I thought, would men ascribe this deadly attribute to women? Clearly, it's about male fear of female sexuality/power. But why is it so persistent? I wondered if, by obscuring the original myth—and with it, the male fear behind it—we perpetuate that fear, because what we feel only subconsciously can be insidious. What I wanted to do in *Teeth* was expose the myth, reveal the absurdity of it, and in so doing, diffuse its power.

And in my telling, I turn the myth on its head: Rather than the woman being the monster who must be tamed by a hero, Dawn is the heroine, and her bodily anomaly is a superpower.

Michael and Anna were fresh out of NYU when I met with them to hear their idea about a stage musical adaptation of *Teeth*. I didn't know their work—I'm not sure they had worked outside of university yet—but I got caught up in their enthusiasm and in their evident sense of humor, which signaled to me that their approach wouldn't be conventionally didactic. And frankly, unlike a straight stage version or a movie sequel, a musical was way out of my wheelhouse, something I could never do myself.

Their talent was revealed to me in their very first workshop presentation. I loved how in-your-face their take was in every respect. It was very different from the movie's tone, which is quite demure (excepting moments of blood-pulsing gore).

In developing the screenplay into the story they wanted to tell, Anna and Michael, like all writers, had to diverge from the source material. Two instances of that divergence that really excited me were the ways in which they reinvented the characters of Brad and Ryan. In my screenplay, Brad as a little boy is smitten with toddler Dawn, but when his father marries Dawn's mother, his love for his now-stepsister becomes taboo. As they grow into their teens, Brad's obsession with Dawn intensifies, and his long-thwarted love/lust turns him into an angry and antisocial young man. He becomes convinced that Dawn's devotion to sexual purity is just a defense against the lust she feels mutually for him. In contrast, Michael and Anna's Brad has no love for his stepsister. His anger stems from the encounter he had as a young boy with Dawn's *vagina dentata*, and that trauma turned him into a woman-fearing incel.

Michael and Anna's Ryan is gay but very conflicted about it, and that figures into his betrayal of Dawn. On both stage and screen, Ryan appears to be a good guy who risks his life to be the hero in the *vagina dentata* myth by bravely having sex with Dawn to conquer her teeth. In the movie, Dawn finds out that the real reason Ryan is having sex with her is to win a bet he made with his friend, about which he brags mid-coitus. In the musical, Ryan's ulterior motive is to prove to the world he is no longer gay, and he does this by live streaming their copulation to the world.

But there was another divergence from the screenplay that I wasn't so excited about—at first. In the musical's final moments, Dawn becomes a villain. And I wasn't sure that I liked "my" heroine becoming a villain. It took me some time and several viewings to realize the genius of this twist.

Where the film ends with the cheer-inducing moment of Dawn fully recognizing her newfound power, Michael and Anna take her story a step or two further, to what is perhaps its logical conclusion. In the musical's last scenes, we cheer Dawn's victories, but in its very final moments those cheers stick in our throats. I won't say much more, so as not to fully spoil the musical's twist ending, but the story becomes a cautionary tale about power and to whom we give it. It's a dark and very timely statement, and a reflection of how far we've come—for good and ill—since 2007.

MITCHELL LICHTENSTEIN is a filmmaker, producer, and actor. In addition to *Teeth*, he made the gothic drama *Angelica*, an adaptation of the novel by Arthur Phillips; the dramedy *Happy Tears*, starring Parker Posey and Demi Moore; and the autobiographical, wordless short drama *Resurrection*. As an actor, he costarred in Robert Altman's *Streamers* (Venice Film Festival Award, Volpi Cup for Best Actor) and Ang Lee's *The Wedding Banquet* (Independent Spirit Award Nomination, Best Male Lead). On stage, he performed in *Anteroom* by Harry Kondoleon at Playwrights Horizons, *The Marriage of Bette & Boo* by Christopher Durang at LATC, and the Broadway debut of *Suddenly Last Summer* (1995) by, of course, Tennessee Williams. The dark comedy *STORIENTED* is Mitchell's first foray into playwriting. He is a graduate of Bennington College (BA) and the Yale School of Drama (MFA). mlichtenstein.com

ACKNOWLEDGMENTS

Mitchell Lichtenstein, Mark Gordon Pictures, LD Entertainment, Baseline Theatrical, Playwrights Horizons, Sarah Benson, Raja Feather Kelley, Julie McBride, Kris Kukul, Patrick Sulken, Noah Teplin, Ars Nova, the NYU Graduate Musical Theatre Writing program, Musical Theatre Factory, Sundance Theatre Lab, the Eugene O'Neill Theater Center, the National Alliance for Musical Theatre, Derek Zasky, Emma Feiwel, David Berlin, Marlo Hunter, Portia Krieger, Luke Redmond, Lenny Redmond, Eli Redmond, Kent Nicholson, Meg Zervoulis, Lynne Shankel, Alexander Gemignani, Shakina Nayfack, Tori Amos, Katie Gamelli, and Alyse Alan Louis.

TEETH

PRODUCTION HISTORY

Teeth had its world premiere at Playwrights Horizons (Adam Greenfield, Artistic Director; Leslie Marcus, Managing Director) in New York on March 19, 2024, presented by special arrangement with Mark Gordon Pictures and LD Entertainment, and with generous support from The Frederick Loewe Foundation and The Rea Charitable Trust. It was directed by Sarah Benson. The scenic design was by Adam Rigg, the costume design was by Enver Chakartash, the lighting design was by Jane Cox and Stacey Derosier, the sound design was by Palmer Hefferan, the sound effect design was by Jeremy Chernick, the orchestrations were by Kris Kukul, the choreography was by Raja Feather Kelly; the music director was Patrick Sulken, the music supervisor was Julie McBride, the intimacy director was Crista Marie Jackson, the fight director was Robert Westley, and the production stage manager was Amanda Spooner. The cast was:

DAWN O'KEEFE	Alyse Alan Louis
PASTOR BILL O'KEEFE/DR. GODFREY	Steven Pasquale
BRAD O'KEEFE	Will Connolly
TOBEY	Jason Gotay
RYAN	Jared Loftin
PROMISE KEEPER GIRL KEKE	Helen J. Shen
PROMISE KEEPER GIRL TRISHA	Jenna Rose Husli

PROMISE KEEPER GIRL FIONA	Phoenix Best
PROMISE KEEPER GIRL STEPHANIE	Wren Rivera
PROMISE KEEPER GIRL RACHAEL	Lexi Rhoades
PROMISE KEEPER GIRL BECKY	Courtney Bassett

This production of *Teeth* transferred to New World Stages (Elliot Greene, CEO of The Shubert Organization) in New York City and opened on October 31, 2024. The production team remained the same, with the following changes: wig, hair, and makeup design were by Rob Pickens and Katie Gell; the production stage manager was Thomas Dieter. The cast remained the same, with the following changes.

PASTOR BILL/DR. GODFREY	Andy Karl
PROMISE KEEPER GIRL KEKE	Madison McBride
PROMISE KEEPER GIRL FIONA	Sydney Parra
PROMISE KEEPER GIRL RACHAEL	Micaela Lamas

Teeth was originally developed at Musical Theatre Factory (Brisa Areli Muñoz, Artistic Director). *Teeth* was further developed with support from the following organizations: Ars Nova (Jason Eagan, Founding Artistic Director); the 2016 Sundance Institute Theatre Lab (Michelle Satter, Founding Senior Director of Sundance Institute's Artist Programs) at MASS MoCA (Joseph C. Thompson, Director); and the 2018 Eugene O'Neill Theater Center's National Music Theater Conference (Preston Whiteway, CEO/Producer; Alexander Gemignani, Conference Artistic Director). *Teeth* was presented at the National Alliance for Musical Theatre's (Betsy King Militello, Executive Director) Festival of New Musicals in 2019 (Pamela Adams and Yuvika Tolani, Festival Co-Chairs).

CHARACTERS

DAWN: Sixteen. An evangelical Christian girl with strong convictions but a good heart. Leader of a teen chastity group called the Promise Keeper Girls.

PASTOR: Late forties, early fifties. Dawn's charismatic but extremely pious stepfather.

BRAD: Seventeen. Dawn's stepbrother and Pastor's biological son. Smart and perceptive, but also very lost and lonely.

TOBEY: Dawn's hot but religiously convicted boyfriend. The actor playing Tobey doubles as other incidental male characters as necessary.

RYAN: A young, technologically savvy, closeted gay teen who attends New Testament Village. The actor playing Ryan doubles as other incidental male characters as necessary.

DR. GODFREY: Late forties, early fifties. A local gynecologist. Doubled by the actor portraying Pastor.

PROMISE KEEPER GIRLS: Keke, Becky, Stephanie, Trisha, Rachael and Fiona. A diverse group of young women with myriad body and personality types who attend New Testament Village.

TRUTHSEEKERS: A geographically diverse group of disaffected young men with myriad body and personality types who belong to an online community where they seek connection in a world they feel is misandrist.

GODFATHER: A charismatic Australian online influencer who leads the Truthseekers on a platform called TruthSeeker Premium. He is only ever heard and not seen.

SETTING

A town called Eden. A church called New Testament Village. Present day, but not heavy-handedly so.

AUTHORS' NOTE

Teeth is a horror musical that explores the breadth of one young woman's experience of sexual repression, shame, desire, and misogyny, which leads to violence that is visited upon her, and which she visits upon others. Why and how she arrives at that violence (and where it ultimately leads her) is as important as why and how the male characters she encounters arrive at the misogyny and violence they visit upon her (and where that ultimately leads them). In *Teeth*, we explore the notion that beneath much of the violence in the world lies an ideological belief that it is necessary. Though there is much fun to be had with blood, jump scares, and penile amputations, it is our intention that the marriage of ideology and violence be the primary delivery system for the many horrors within.

SONGS

Song	Performers
Precious Gift	*Dawn, Promise Keeper Girls*
Between Her Thighs	*Brad, Truthseekers*
Modest Is Hottest	*Tobey, Dawn, Promise Keeper Girls*
Shame in My Body	*Dawn, Promise Keeper Girls*
A Real Man	*Pastor, Brad*
Playing with Fire	*Tobey, Dawn, Promise Keeper Girls*
Born Again	*Ryan, Dawn, Promise Keeper Girls*
When She Gave Birth	*Promise Keeper Girls*
Teeth	*Pastor, Brad, Promise Keeper Girls, Truthseekers*
Always the Woman	*Dawn, Promise Keeper Girls*
Shame in My Body (Reprise)	*Dawn*
Girls Like You	*Dr. Godfrey, Dawn, Promise Keeper Girls*
According to the Wiki	*Ryan, Brad, Truthseekers*
I'm Your Guy	*Ryan, Dawn*
When She Gave Birth (Reprise)	*Promise Keeper Girls*
Dentata	*All Company*
Take Me Down	*All Company*

SCENE ONE

Curtain rises on the New Testament Village church sanctuary, present day. Brad and Dawn O'Keefe stand facing each other, as though they are facing off. Eventually, Brad and Dawn move to their seats on opposite sides of the congregation.

The tableau suddenly snaps to life. Pastor Bill O'Keefe moves center to the pulpit. Dawn is rapt and attentive. Brad is zoned out. Ryan records/films.

PASTOR: Now! The Bible tells us that the serpent was more subtle than any beast of the field. And when he said unto woman, "shall ye not eat of every tree in the garden," she was tempted and ate the fruit that Father God *COMMANDED* her not to eat, bringing about *the fall of man* when she shared the apple with him. Because their eyes opened to the realization that they were *NAKED*! *SEXUAL! So what did they do?* They covered themselves with fig leaves, ashamed. Which brings us to the burning question New Testament Village young women must answer today in light of recent events, and that question is: Woman? Where is your fig leaf? Woman? Where is your shame? I'm gonna ask that again!

(Aggressively confronting Dawn and the Promise Keeper Girls) WOMAN? WHERE IS YOUR FIG LEAF? WOMAN? WHERE IS YOUR SHAME?!?

(Seeing Brad zoning out, Pastor confronts him and startles him to attention.)

Wake up, Brad! Do you think the fall of man doesn't have anything to do with you?!?

BRAD: Yes, Pastor! I'm sorry, Pastor! I—

PASTOR: Ryan, how many are watching at home?

RYAN: Fourteen hundred and climbing on New Testament Village's live stream right now, Pastor!

PASTOR: Amen-amen. Because it's time to confront the elephant in the room.

(The room bristles.)

Keke, who is that elephant?

KEKE: Amy Sue Pearson!

PASTOR: Amy Sue Pearson! And why is Amy Sue such an elephant, Trisha?

TRISHA: Because Amy Sue got herself pregnant!

PASTOR: Ding, ding, ding! Because Amy Sue got herself pregnant! And how did Amy Sue get herself pregnant, Fiona?

FIONA: By letting Brock Matthews put his penis in her vagina!

PASTOR: By letting Brock Matthews put his nasty little penis in her vagina! And why would Amy Sue go and do a thing like that, Stephanie?

STEPHANIE: Because she let The Enemy corrupt her mind!

PASTOR: Because she let The Enemy corrupt her mind! And Rachael, how on Earth could Amy Sue let The Enemy corrupt her mind?

RACHAEL: Because she gave up on the promise! Because she gave up on the ring!

PASTOR: But you're New Testament Village Promise Keeper Girls, Becky! You're not from the secular world! You were born and raised here in *Eden*, where young women carry the banner for an especially *awesome* message of female empowerment through sexual purity until marriage or *death*. And why would Amy Sue just flush her banner down the crapper and let the serpent of temptation slither inside her, Becky?

BECKY: Because it felt good!

PASTOR: No, Becky! Feeling good is a *lie*. It's a lie, it's a lie—

DAWN: IT'S A LIE!

PROMISE KEEPER GIRLS, RYAN AND TOBEY: IT'S A LIE!

PASTOR: That's right! And it's a lie that Amy Sue told under *your* PKG leadership, Dawn.

DAWN: Yes, Pastor. I know she did. I take full responsibility, but I would *never* condone—

PASTOR: No "buts," Dawn. Not today. Not when it comes to the fall of man. Because you wouldn't want what happened to Brock to happen to your little boyfriend Tobey here because of your "but," would you?

TOBEY: No way, Pastor! Nope!

DAWN: Never, never—

(Pastor drags a chair to the front of the church before Dawn can interrupt.)

PASTOR: Then what do you say to any other Promise Keeper Girls who might be thinking about "feeling good"?

PRECIOUS GIFT

DAWN: I say, Promise Keeper Girls can't be about *feeling* good! I say, Promise Keeper Girls have to be about *being* good!!!

PASTOR: Amen-amen! That's my perfect little baby girl, but don't tell me! Tell her! Tell Amy Sue! 'Cause it's "Precious Gift" time, church!

(The NTV congregation cheers and Brad groans.)

So get off your "buts," look that girl in the eye, and remind her who you are!

(PKG cheers Dawn on—"Go, Dawn!" "You got this!" etc.)

DAWN *(To an imaginary Amy Sue)*:

AS PROMISE KEEPER GIRLS, WE VOW TO KEEP OUR VIRTUE
WITH THIS RING UPON OUR FINGERS, WE ABSTAIN

PASTOR: Yep!

DAWN:

AS PROMISE KEEPER GIRLS, WE CLEAVE TO HIGHER STANDARDS
WE DON'T FLINCH, WE PROUDLY GO AGAINST THE GRAIN
WE'RE IN THE WORLD, WE'RE IN THE WORLD, NOT OF IT
WHILE OTHER GIRLS ARE SPIRITUALLY ADRIFT
THEY SEE THEIR MAIDENHEADS AS NOTHING BUT A BURDEN
BUT TO US IT'S SUCH A PRECIOUS, PRECIOUS GIFT

DAWN AND PROMISE KEEPER GIRLS:

A PRECIOUS GIFT

BECKY:

THAT'S ONLY FOR A HUSBAND!

DAWN AND PROMISE KEEPER GIRLS:

A PRECIOUS GIFT

RACHAEL:

THAT COMES WRAPPED IN A BOW!

DAWN AND PROMISE KEEPER GIRLS:

A PRECIOUS GIFT

TRISHA:

WITH NO RETURNS OR EXCHANGES!

DAWN AND PROMISE KEEPER GIRLS:

A PRECIOUS GIFT WE GET JUST ONE CHANCE TO BESTOW!

FIONA:

AS PROMISE KEEPER GIRLS, WE'RE SOLIDERS IN BATTLE
WITH THIS RING, WE SALLY FORTH TO WIN THE WAR

KEKE:

HIS WORD IS VERY CLEAR, HE GAVE US TWO CHOICES
TAKE YOUR PICK—ARE YOU A VIRGIN OR A WHORE?

DAWN AND PROMISE KEEPER GIRLS:

THANK GOD FOR JESUS! THANK GOD FOR JESUS!
HIS BLOOD IS LIKE PURE HONEY ON MY LIPS!
THE GIFT HE GAVE US! THE GIFT HE GAVE US!
STAYS LOCKED UP TIGHT IN A BOX AT THE
MEETING OF MY HIPS!
A PRECIOUS GIFT!

TRISHA AND FIONA:

THAT'S NOT TO BE DEFILED!

DAWN AND PROMISE KEEPER GIRLS:

A PRECIOUS GIFT

BECKY AND RACHAEL:

IT'S WHAT SETS ME APART!

DAWN AND PROMISE KEEPER GIRLS:

A PRECIOUS GIFT

STEPHANIE:

MY SHINY LITTLE DIAMOND!

DAWN AND PROMISE KEEPER GIRLS:

A PRECIOUS GIFT IS NOT LIKE SUSHI *À LA CARTE*!

DAWN *(To an imaginary Amy Sue)*:

YOU'RE A PROMISE KEEPER GIRL WHO DARED TO
BREAK THE PROMISE
SO OUR JUDGMENT UPON YOU MUST BE SWIFT
MAY YOU ALWAYS FEEL THE MISERY
THE COLD AND THE DARKNESS
THAT COMES FROM GIVING UP
YOUR PRECIOUS GIFT

PROMISE KEEPER GIRLS:

AH

DAWN AND PROMISE KEEPER GIRLS:

PRECIOUS GIFT!

BRAD: I need some air.

PASTOR: It's "Precious Gift" time, Brad. Sit down.

PROMISE KEEPER GIRLS:

A PRECIOUS GIFT
THAT SHE TOOK FOR GRANTED!

DAWN:

SHE TOOK IT FOR GRANTED!

PROMISE KEEPER GIRLS:

A PRECIOUS GIFT
THAT SHE PASSED AROUND!

DAWN:

AND AROUND AND AROUND!

PROMISE KEEPER GIRLS:

A PRECIOUS GIFT
SHE ABUSED AND DISCARDED!

DAWN:

AND DISCARDED!

PROMISE KEEPER GIRLS:

A PRECIOUS GIFT
FOR HER BOYFRIEND TO POUND!

DAWN:

BETWEEN MY LEGS!

PROMISE KEEPER GIRLS:

A PRECIOUS GIFT
YOU BLESSED US WITH A VULVA!

DAWN:

BETWEEN MY LEGS, GOD!

PROMISE KEEPER GIRLS:

A PRECIOUS GIFT
YOU CURSE US WITH IT TOO!

DAWN:

BY DAY!

PROMISE KEEPER GIRLS:

BY DAY!

DAWN:

BY NIGHT!

PROMISE KEEPER GIRLS:

BY NIGHT!

DAWN:

WE'RE PROMISE KEEPER GIRLS WHO FIGHT

DAWN AND PROMISE KEEPER GIRLS:

THOUGH AT TIMES IT'S SUCH A HEAVY,
HEAVY LIFT

DAWN:

BUT I WILL

PROMISE KEEPER GIRLS:

I WILL

DAWN:

NOT FLEE

PROMISE KEEPER GIRLS:

NOT FLEE

DAWN:

YOU EMPOWER ME
IN THE NAME

PROMISE KEEPER GIRLS:

IN THE NAME

DAWN:

IN THE NAME OF MY PRECIOUS, PRECIOUS GIFT!

PROMISE KEEPER GIRLS:

WHITE WEDDING KEEP MY LEGS CLOSED, JESUS WANTS ME FOR A SUNBEAM!

DAWN:

PRECIOUS GIFT!

PROMISE KEEPER GIRLS:

NO COVETING MY NEIGHBOR'S ASS, NO REACHING FOR HIS FIG LEAF!

DAWN:

PRECIOUS GIFT!

PROMISE KEEPER GIRLS:

HAIL MARY, PRAY TO KILL THE SERPENT COILED UP INSIDE ME!

DAWN AND PROMISE KEEPER GIRLS:

AS DAUGHTERS OF GOD WE WOULD PLUCK OUT
OUR EYES BEFORE WE WOULD SURRENDER
OUR PRECIOUS, PRECIOUS GIFT!

(Dawn knocks over the chair. Everyone except Brad cheers and jumps to their feet.)

PASTOR: Precious gift!!! Amen-amen! Pluck! Out!

(All but Brad help Pastor finish his sentence.)

ALL: Your! *Eyyyyyes!*

PASTOR: Yes, Promise Keeper Girls! You cannot enter the gates of Heaven unless you keep the gates of Hell . . .

(Dawn helps Pastor finish his sentence.)

PASTOR AND DAWN: *Clooooosed!!!!*

PASTOR: Until we meet again, NTV live streamers! *(To the audience congregation, jocular)* The rest of you, *get outta here*!

(Pastor goes to chat with some of PKG. Ryan begins to pack up his equipment.)

DAWN *(Crossing to Brad, trying to charm him)*: Hey, Brad! You were lookin' good bustin' a move during "Precious Gift" over he—

BRAD: Get away! Get away! Don't touch me!

(Brad shrinks from her touch and exits, disgusted. Pastor joins Dawn.)

PASTOR: Hey! What was that about? What's wrong with that boy now?

DAWN: I don't know, Pastor. I was just trying to connect with him.

PASTOR: Brad's just jealous. 'Cause even though you're not my biological child and he is, the two of us could not be more bonded by the blood of the lamb.

DAWN: Well, whatever it is, I just wanna *help him*. Because it's obvious he's in a lot of pain.

PASTOR: That's just manhood, Dawn. He'll either conquer the pain or it'll conquer him. C'mon, let's go home.

(Pastor, Dawn and PKG exit as Brad enters a virtual meeting platform called TruthSeeker Premium. Other boys and men join him, wearing VR headsets and listening to Godfather, a popular online men's life coach. We only ever hear his disembodied voice. He's Australian.)

GODFATHER: There's a pain all men carry, Truthseekers. Some of us carry it in our shoulders. Some in our stomachs. Some of us even carry it in our balls—in our nutsacks. It's a pain we've become numb to in this era of "dismantling the patriarchy." As though the patriarchy isn't the one thing protecting society from the chaos of the animals. But oh no, now we can't even sit on a bloody train without being "manspreaders" for Christ's sake! Because we *take up too much space*! Do you see, Truthseekers? This pain is not really ours. It was given to us by *the feminocracy*. Savage, lonely females we have allowed to domesticate us. To save our species from extinction, we must transform into high-value men. To find out how, click on TruthSeeker Premium. And don't forget to smash that like button, as it really helps with the algorithm! Seek the truth and be free!

TRUTHSEEKERS: Seek the truth and be free!

TRUTHSEEKER #1: The feminocracy! Holy fuck! Godfather is so fuckin' based! Where do you guys feel your pain? I feel my pain in my neck.

(The other Truthseekers acknowledge his pain.)

TRUTHSEEKER #3: I feel mine in my lower back.

(The other Truthseekers acknowledge his pain.)

TRUTHSEEKER #2: My pain's in my hip flexor usually.

(The other Truthseekers acknowledge his pain. Brad nervously speaks up.)

BRAD: My pain is in my finger. I think it comes from my step-sister's cunt.

TRUTHSEEKER #3: Say what?

TRUTHSEEKER #2: Looks like we've got a new Truthseeker, Truthseekers.

TRUTHSEEKERS: Hey, Truthseeker!

BRAD: Oh, hey there, guys. Nice to meet you, my name is—

TRUTHSEEKER #1: No civilian names, bro. We're just Truth-seekers here.

BRAD: Oh. Well, I'm a longtime lurker and I decided to dive into TruthSeeker Premium after I saw Godfather was going to be talking about male pain. Nobody cares about my pain. Especially not Pastor. Pastor's my dad. But he made me stop calling him that after my mom ran off, which frankly I don't blame her for 'cause Pastor's psychotic. See, he's got this thing about sexual purity and women and I'm talking too much, I'm talking too much, I'm sorry I—

TRUTHSEEKER #1: Truthseeker, it's okay. Sometimes a guy just needs to talk. You're safe here. Speak.

TRUTHSEEKER #2: Yeah. 'Cause if the feminocracy hurt you in your finger, we *really* gotta know what *that's* about.

TRUTHSEEKER #3: And did I mishear, or did you say it was your *stepsister* who hurt you with her *cunt*?

(Brad begins to tell the truth. It's a "power" that the Truthseekers begin to feel.)

BRAD: Yeah, when I was like six or seven and she was a year younger. We were just messing around in a kiddie pool that Pastor and Dawn's mother, Kim, had put out for us. And Dawn dared me to take my swimsuit down, and I dared her to take hers down, so we both took our swimsuits down and were, you know, naked, so then Dawn asked me if she could touch mine and I was scared to let her touch mine down there, so I told her she had to let me touch hers down there first . . . but when I did—

(Brad's truth causes a mystical online empathy to possess the Truthseekers and they cry out, feeling Brad's pain in their fingers, absorbing this memory.)

TRUTHSEEKERS: Ahhhhhh!

TRUTHSEEKER #2: Jesus, the pain! I can actually *feel* your pain, Truthseeker!

TRUTHSEEKER #1: I can *see* your six-year-old hand!

TRUTHSEEKER #3: I can smell your blood gushing into the water!

TRUTHSEEKER #2: Then Pastor scoops Dawn into his loving arms—

TRUTHSEEKER #3: Even as you bleed and tell him about the pain—

TRUTHSEEKER #1: But all Pastor cares about is that you dared to touch Dawn's muff!

BRAD: Yes! And after that, it was like it never happened. I used to feel the pain in my finger whenever Dawn came near me, but over time I learned how to suppress it so that it would just go . . .

BRAD AND TRUTHSEEKERS: Numb.

BETWEEN HER THIGHS

BRAD: But then, today at NTV, I felt it again and it hit me after all these years, clear as day.

TRUTHSEEKER #3: What hit you, Truthseekeer?

BRAD:

SHE BIT ME
IT BIT ME
BETWEEN HER PUSSY LIPS
I FELT A TWINGE OF PRESSURE, THEN SUCH PAIN
I YANKED MY HAND AND SAW THAT I HAD JUST
FOUR FINGERTIPS
I SCREAMED LIKE I HAD TRULY GONE INSANE

SHE BIT ME
IT BIT ME
HER COOTER ISN'T PURE
THIS ISN'T SPECULATION, LET'S BE CLEAR
AND THOUGH I HAVE NO OTHER PROOF, THE
PAIN THAT I ENDURE
IT'S PROOF AND CONFIRMATION OF MY FEAR

WHO IS SHE UNDERNEATH HER SKIN?
WHAT LURKS BEHIND HER EYES?

WHERE ARE HER FANGS AND TENTACLES?
WHEN WILL HER DARK MOON RISE?
SHE HIDES BEHIND VIRGINITY
IT'S JUST A CHEAP DISGUISE
'CAUSE THE TRUTH IS HIDDEN IN BETWEEN
HER THIGHS

TRUTHSEEKER #2: It's like this news article I just found about an ancient bacterium that got into the water supply of this small, remote village in Japan and caused a gynecological mutation in all their women! And get this: not long after the outbreak, all the males in the village disappeared!

BRAD: That's freaky, but what does it have to do with Dawn, Truthseeker?

TRUTHSEEKER #2:

IT BIT YOU
SHE BIT YOU
BUT IS IT ONLY HER?
WHAT IF IT'S MORE LIKE ALL OF WOMANKIND?

TRUTHSEEKERS #1 AND #3:

A COVEN FULL OF SUCCUBI
SO FOUL AND SINISTER

TRUTHSEEKERS:

MEDUSAS WITH THE POWER TO SPELLBIND

BRAD:

WHO ARE THEY UNDERNEATH THEIR SKIN?
WHAT LURKS BEHIND THEIR EYES?
WHERE ARE THEIR FANGS AND TENTACLES?
WHEN WILL THEIR DARK MOONS RISE?

BRAD AND TRUTHSEEKERS:

WHY TREAT THESE GIRLS LIKE HAPPY MEALS
PACKED WITH SOME SPECIAL PRIZE
WHEN THERE'S PROBABLY DANGER IN BETWEEN
THEIR THIGHS?

(Dawn enters.)

DAWN: Hey, Brad, you got a minute?

(Brad takes off his VR headset. The Truthseekers recede.)

BRAD: I'm kinda busy!

DAWN: Oh. Sorry. I just wanted to check in. How's your heart?

BRAD: How's my *heart*?

DAWN: Yeah. 'Cause you seemed kinda upset when you left NTV today.

BRAD: There was a lot to be upset about.

DAWN: Anything in particular?

BRAD: What do you want, Dawn?

DAWN: I was just thinking you might be feeling a little left out, considering everything going on with Amy Sue.

BRAD: I'm more than happy to be left out of that insanity, to be honest.

DAWN: And another thing I was thinking you might need to hear is that being pure is a precious gift for boys too, you know.

BRAD: What?!?

DAWN: It's a precious gift for boys because before Eve tempted him, Adam was a virgin too, and he was highly favored by Father God, so there's nothing wrong with you either, Brad.

BRAD: Okay you literally sound like a pod person with this stuff, but since you wanna get into it: I actually think there's *plenty* wrong with me, virgin or not.

DAWN: I'm not trying to embarrass you. I just want you to know that *I see you*.

BRAD: And yet I never see *you* when Pastor's wailing on *me* with his belt.

DAWN: I don't love how hard Pastor is on you, but he's just trying to help you find your ministry, like he helped me find mine with PKG!

BRAD: And that's another thing! Who are you to judge Amy Sue, given what streetwalkin' shenanigans *your mom* was up to before she married Pastor and "got saved"?

DAWN: That's low, Brad! My mom loved you! And whatever her past was, she isn't even alive to defend herself! Why are you being so hostile all of a sudden?

BRAD: I'm just following my ministry! Seeking the truth!

(Brad holds his scarred finger in her face aggressively.)

And *this* is my truth, Dawn! Remember?!?

DAWN *(Overlapping)*: What? No! What are you talking about?!?

BRAD *(Overlapping)*: You bit me! In the backyard! *Stop pretending!*

DAWN *(Overlapping)*: Bit you?!? I didn't bite—

(Brad grabs at Dawn but she dodges him, pulling away, shocked.)

BRAD: *It* bit me! Yes, you did! Down there!

DAWN: Down there?!? What?!? You can't talk to me like that!

BRAD *(Overlapping)*: Yes! That's right! Why not? It's true!

DAWN *(Overlapping)*: I can't believe you would *joke* about something so dis[gusting]—

BRAD: I'm not joking!

DAWN: Then you're crazy!!! I'm sorry I even bothered coming in here! And Becky was right! You *do* smell!

(Dawn exits. Brad puts back on his VR headset and the Truthseekers return.)

BRAD: Well, fuck Becky too! Now *I know* I'm right!

BRAD:	TRUTHSEEKERS:
THEY FEAR US UNDERNEATH	
THEIR SKIN	
I SAW IT IN DAWN'S EYES	
I SMELL IT ALL THROUGH PKG	OH
A STENCH THEY CAN'T DISGUISE	OH

BRAD AND TRUTHSEEKERS:

THE WEAKER SEX HAS WEAKENED US
AND CUT US DOWN TO SIZE
BUT IF WE PUSH BACK WITH ALL OUR MIGHT
CAN WE WIN THIS EXISTENTIAL FIGHT?
CAN WE DESTROY WHAT THEY'RE HIDING?
WHAT FEMINOCRACY'S HIDING

BRAD:

IN BETWEEN THEIR THIGHS

I bet Godfather will know.

TRUTHSEEKERS: Yeah . . .

SCENE TWO

The Promise Keeper Girls sit in a circle in the NTV sanctuary. Dawn carefully listens to their responses to a question she has posed.

KEKE: Okay well, I wanna marry a guy who makes me feel protected!

(They all cheer in agreement.)

TRISHA: I wanna marry a guy who loves me like Christ loves the church!

(They all cheer in agreement.)

STEPHANIE: I wanna marry a guy who never asks me to take the trash out!

(They all laugh and cheer in agreement.)

RACHAEL: I wanna marry a guy who tells me the truth even when I don't want to hear it!

(They all cheer in agreement.)

FIONA: I wanna marry a guy who is truly my best friend!

(They all "awww" and cheer in agreement.)

BECKY: Well, I wanna marry a guy who could be as much of a cutie-patootie captain of the Eden High Crossbearers basketball team as Tobey is!

(They all "awww" and cheer in agreement. Tobey enters, unseen by the girls.)

DAWN: Okay so now that we've gotten *those* pancakes on the griddle, let's flip 'em over. Because what difference does it make the kind of guy *you* wanna marry if *you're* not the kind of girl worth being married to?

(This hits PKG hard.)

Trisha, are you worth being married to? Becky? Are *any* of you worthy of your future husbands' last names? Have you sat with Father God and done a personal inventory lately? Because if you haven't, it won't be long before you've joined the coven of fallen women along with Amy Sue. And all because you thought a little boy-craziness wasn't a big deal. And that was just me tempting you with an "innocent" little question about a hypothetical guy. What are you gonna do when *The Enemy* comes knocking at your kitchen door with something real? *(Pause)* Yeah.

Do you see now? That's how fast these little pancakes burn, PKG.

TRISHA: That's heavy.

BECKY: That's *really* heavy!

TOBEY: It's heavy for us guys too.

(PKG reacts to Tobey's presence in the room.)

DAWN: Hey, PKG? How about we take a beat to reset and come back in ten? *(Trying to cheer up the despondent PKG)* And don't beat yourselves up too much, PKG; we're all in this together.

(PKG exits. Tobey gives Dawn a chaste physical greeting.)

Hi.

TOBEY: Hi. Everything good here?

DAWN: We've got a lot more growing up to do, but we'll get there. How was basketball practice? How did it go with Brock?

TOBEY: It was a disaster. There was a whole scene on the basketball court when me and the guys confronted him about his situation with Amy Sue, and I *lost* it on him. It got really ugly.

DAWN: Nobody was hurt, were they? Is Brock okay? Are you okay?

MODEST IS HOTTEST

TOBEY: I'm fine, everybody's fine. Coach broke it up before it could get out of hand. But this whole thing just got me thinking about you and me, and about how all I want is to be worthy of being with a girl as perfect as *you* are.

DAWN: Tobey, I'm not perfect!

TOBEY: Yeah you are! 'Cause compared to you, even the most sanctified girls at my last church were total *hoochie moms*! But between your commitment to the Village and PKG, the way you carry yourself—heck, even the way you dress. Dawn, you're the whole darn package!

YOU DON'T ROCK TANK TOPS AND "BOOTY
SHORTS"
YOU DON'T INVITE THE EYE TO ASK FOR MORE
YOU DON'T WEAR SKIRTS ABOVE THE KNEE
YOU DRESS WITH CLASS AND MODESTY
SOME GIRLS GO OUT WITH PANTS THAT CLING
YOU WON'T LEAVE HOME WITHOUT YOUR
PURITY RING
YOU DON'T TEMPT FATE WITH SPAGHETTI
STRAPS
YOU'RE A GIRL WHO KEEPS IT ALL UNDER WRAPS,
'CAUSE

MODEST IS HOTTEST
MODEST IS HOTTEST
UNDERNEATH IT ALL, SAFE AND SUSPENDED
MODEST IS HOTTEST
MODEST IS HOTTEST
RIGHT UNDER MY NOSE, THE WAY GOD
INTENDED
MODEST IS HOTTEST
MODEST IS HOTTEST
DRESSED SO MY EYES ARE NEVER OFFENDED
I'M KIND OF OBSESSED WHEN IT COMES TO
YOUR MODESTY

DAWN:

I LOVE YOUR SINGLE-MINDEDNESS
WHEN GOD SAYS GO, YOU ALWAYS ACQUIESCE
YOU HIDE HIS WORD INSIDE OF YOU
YOU'RE A RIGHTEOUS MAN IN ALL YOU SAY
AND DO
THAT'S HOLY MASCULINITY
THAT'S YOUR CORE, YOUR LOCK AND YOUR KEY
SOME GUYS WOULD PUSH FOR MORE FROM ME
BUT NOT YOU, 'CAUSE YOU STILL AGREE THAT

MODEST IS HOTTEST
MODEST IS HOTTEST
NOT ONLY FOR SHOW, AND NOT AN ILLUSION
MODEST IS HOTTEST
MODEST IS HOTTEST
EVERYWHERE YOU GO, A FOREGONE
CONCLUSION
MODEST IS HOTTEST
MODEST IS HOTTEST
HOW YOU STEER CLEAR OF ANY CONFUSION
I THANK FATHER GOD FOR YOUR LOVE OF MY
MODESTY

TOBEY:

YOU'RE A BEAUTY
SO MY DUTY
IS TO TREAT YOUR LOVE LIKE GLASS
IT EXCITES ME
AND IGNITES ME
TO THE POINT OF CRITICAL MASS

(PKG sneaks back in and eavesdrops.)

TOBEY:	PROMISE KEEPER GIRLS:
MODEST IS HOTTEST	AH!
MODEST IS HOTTEST	AH!
IT'S LIKE CHRISTMAS DAY	
ANTICIPATION	ANTICIPATION!
MODEST IS HOTTEST	AH!
MODEST IS HOTTEST	AH!
FIRST A SLIGHT DELAY,	THEN
THEN GRATIFICATION	GRATIFICATION!
MODEST IS HOTTEST	AH!
MODEST IS HOTTEST	AH!
HOTTER THAN "H" IN MY	"H"
IMAGINATION	IMAGINATION!

(PKG exits.)

TOBEY:

I'M JUST SO OBSESSED WHEN IT COMES TO YOUR MODESTY

DAWN:

YOUR GODLINESS MAKES ME FEEL SO SECURE

TOBEY:

BUT ALSO SO BLESSED BY YOUR VIRTUE AND MODESTY

DAWN:

IT'S LIKE A NARCOTIC THAT'S TOTALLY PURE

DAWN AND TOBEY:

AND IT TOTALLY, TOTALLY, TOTALLY
TURNS ME ON . . .

TOBEY: Okay, now I need to run home and shower. But would you mind if we meet back here after you're done with PKG?

DAWN: Uh, sure. Is something wrong?

TOBEY: There's a few more things I think I need to unpack with you, if that's okay.

DAWN: Sure, of course.

(They exchange a chaste goodbye and Tobey exits as PKG returns.)

TOBEY: Bye, PKG.

PROMISE KEEPER GIRLS: Bye, Tobey.

FIONA: Dawn, what's wrong? Did something happen with Tobey?

DAWN: No, no, we're fine I think. But the spirit is telling me that we should just take the rest of the day to go home and do our inventories. Before you go though, let's be transparent and accountable to each other about what challenges we're facing. What do you each need to work on?

FIONA: I need to work on my steadfastness.

TRISHA: I need to work on my stubborness.

RACHAEL: My talkativeness.

KEKE: My possessiveness.

STEPHANIE: *My* possessiveness!

BECKY: And I need to work on my . . . secretiveness.

DAWN: Oh, yeah. Secretiveness is the hardest one of all, Becky. Which is why doing these inventories is so important. Because if there's one thing Satan loves, it's what?

PROMISE KEEPER GIRLS: Secrets.

DAWN: And that's because the only place you can hide a secret is where?

PROMISE KEEPER GIRLS: Inside.

DAWN: Inside. That's exactly right. See you next time.

(PKG exits. Dawn does her inventory.)

SHAME IN MY BODY

And what am I gonna work on? Where do I even start?

MY PANTIES ARE WET
BUT IT'S NOT BLOOD OR SWEAT
AND IT'S TOBEY'S DOING
HE'S PURE AND HE'S SWEET
BUT I STILL FEEL THE HEAT
THE HEAT OF TEMPTATION

'CAUSE HE'S SO FREAKIN' HOT
AND I WISH I DID NOT
FEEL DESIRE BREWING
BUT WHEN DESIRE BURNS
THAT'S WHEN SHAME RETURNS
AND I FEEL THE STING OF DAMNATION!

I FEEL THE STING OF SHAME IN MY BODY
I FEEL IT WHIP ME AGAIN
I FEEL THE STING OF SHAME IN MY BODY
I FEEL IT SO DEEPLY WITHIN
I FEEL THE STING OF SHAME IN MY BODY
IT KEEPS AND PROTECTS ME FROM SIN
DESIRE WON'T WIN
AS LONG AS I KEEP WALLOWING IN
THE SHAME IN MY BODY

(The Promise Keeper Girls appear as serpents, attempting to lure Dawn into temptation.)

TRISHA:

DESIRE IS SLICK

RACHAEL:

SHE IS CUNNING AND QUICK

KEKE:

SHE IS MESMERIZING

FIONA:

SHE EBBS AND SHE FLOWS

BECKY:

LEAVES A MESS WHEN SHE GOES

STEPHANIE:

SHE HAS NO DETERRENT

PROMISE KEEPER GIRLS:

SHE ROARS LIKE THE SEA
SHE'S AS WILD AS CAN BE
SHE IS TANTALIZING

DAWN:

AND I HAVE COME UNMOORED
TRIPPING OVERBOARD
AND GOTTEN SWEPT AWAY IN HER CURRENT

SO NOW I'M DROWNING IN THE SHAME IN
MY BODY
'CAUSE I LET MY DESIRE SURGE
I'M DROWNING IN THE SHAME IN MY BODY
AND I MUST COMPLETELY SUBMERGE
BY DROWNING IN THE SHAME IN MY BODY
WHENEVER I COME NEAR THE VERGE OF
CARNAL URGE

PROMISE KEEPER GIRLS:

URGE . . .

DAWN:

'CAUSE A WOMAN'S HOLE LEADS STRAIGHT
TO HELL

PROMISE KEEPER GIRLS:

DESIRE! DESIRE! DESIRE! DESIRE! DESIRE!

DAWN:

IT'S FULL OF LUST WE'RE MEANT TO QUELL

PROMISE KEEPER GIRLS:

DESIRE! DESIRE! DESIRE! DESIRE! DESIRE!

DAWN:

AND HUNGRY LIPS

PROMISE KEEPER GIRLS:

DESIRE

DAWN:

THAT HUM BELOW

PROMISE KEEPER GIRLS:

DESIRE

DAWN:

THE FOUNT OF SHAME

PROMISE KEEPER GIRLS:

DESIRE

DAWN:

A MONTHLY FLOW

PROMISE KEEPER GIRLS:

DESIRE

DAWN:

AND OTHER DARK SECRETS WE PROBABLY DON'T EVEN KNOW

PROMISE KEEPER GIRLS:

OOH! DESIRE! DESIRE! DESIRE! DESIRE! DESIRE . . .

DAWN:

I NEED THE STING OF SHAME IN MY BODY
DESIRE IS SUCH AGONY
I NEED THE STING OF SHAME IN MY BODY
ITS VENOM SPREADS SO PERFECTLY

(PKG slithers and gyrates as the venom of desire builds within their bodies, until they reach a point of climax.)

DAWN:	PROMISE KEEPER GIRLS:
I NEED THE STING OF SHAME IN MY BODY	AH
IT'S SHAME FATHER GOD PUT IN ME	AH
TO SET ME FREE	
FREE FROM TOBEY'S SCENT STILL IN MY NOSE	OOH
FREE FROM WISHING HE'D RIP OFF MY CLOTHES	OOH
AND LICK ME FROM MY HEAD	OOH
DOWN TO MY TOES . . .	OOH, OOH, AH

DAWN:

FREE FROM THE DESIRING THAT FLOWS
ALL THROUGH MY BODY

PROMISE KEEPER GIRLS:

YOUR BODY

(PKG lets out a post-climactic hiss.)

SCENE THREE

Brad's bedroom. In the dark, Brad and the Truthseekers wear their headsets. On TruthSeeker Premium, Godfather speaks to them.

GODFATHER: So if I'm hearing you correctly, you Truthseekers believe this bitch has actual *teeth in her furry taco*? *(A chuckle)* This perfectly illustrates *my point*—that the more we feed the feminocracy, the stronger it becomes. So strong that it can actually cause the male to physically injure himself.

BRAD: But it wasn't *self*-harm, Godfather. *There really was something sharp down there.*

TRUTHSEEKER #1: He's still got a scar where the doctor sewed back his fingertip.

TRUTHSEEKER #2: And we felt it too, Godfather.

GODFATHER: Truthseekers, I assure you: this shared memory is merely a psychosomatic, post-hypnotic suggestion the feminocrats put into your minds. The *false* power they have in the axe wounds between their legs is *nothing* compared to the very *real* power you have in the axes swinging between yours. And that's power you need to reclaim because there's a whole lot of pussy out there, Truthseekers, *and it's not gonna fuck itself.*

BRAD: Okay so if *that's* how we reclaim our power from the feminocracy, where do we start?

GODFATHER: Take off your shirts.

(Somewhat simultaneously, Brad and the Truthseekers are caught by surprise.)

BRAD: Godfather?!?

TRUTHSEEKER #1: What?

TRUTHSEEKER #2: C'mon!

GODFATHER: You can become high-value men, or you can let the teeth you imagine gobble you whole. Now let's get on with it.

BRAD AND TRUTHSEEKERS: Yes, Godfather.

(Brad and the Truthseekers remove their shirts.)

BRAD: Now what?

GODFATHER: *Feel yourself.* Your body. Feel all of it.

(Brad and the Truthseekers reach down into their pants and begin to feel themselves.)

Step into your sexuality and your manhood and roar, Truthseekers.

(Pastor enters and is momentarily stunned by what he sees.)

BRAD: Fuck! This does feel kinda good actually—

PASTOR: Stop doing that! You can't do that!

(As Pastor rips the VR headset from Brad's face, the Truthseekers disappear. Both Pastor and Brad are terrified for different reasons.)

BRAD: Oh God—

PASTOR: How *DARE* you use His holy name that way?!?!? There's *nothing* Godly about touching yourself down there! Oh, Father God *told* me you were up to something wicked in here, but I didn't think you would be . . . Put some clothes on, put some clothes on! What is this?!?

BRAD: My VR headset. I got it online.

PASTOR *(A mix of righteous anger and jealousy)*: This is for looking at *pornography*, isn't it?

BRAD: No, Pastor!

PASTOR: Then what is it?!?

BRAD: Just some research for school.

PASTOR: Liar. Something dark-sided in this contraption told you to touch the meat of Adam and "pleasure" yourself, didn't it?

BRAD: NO!

PASTOR: *Who told you to pleasure yourself*, and you better not lie to me!

BRAD: My VR Godfather says I can't be a high-value man until I feel myself!

PASTOR *(Cries out in almost physical pain)*: Is that what your "VR Godfather" says? Well, what does Exodus Chapter 20, Verse 3 say?

BRAD: "Thou shalt have no other gods before me."

PASTOR: *Louder, so He can hear you!*

BRAD: "THOU SHALT HAVE NO OTHER GODS BEFORE ME!!!"

PASTOR: Amen-amen. So we've got a real problem here. Because my only begotten son is in his bedroom serving false gods and playing with the meat of Adam because he thinks that makes him a "high-value" man. Well, playing with the meat of Adam is for faggots and little children. Being a man is about responsibility. And pain. But you've got *so much* of your mother in you. So much of her *heterodoxy* and her *perverse* curiosity! Like the time you tried to eat of the fruit between Dawn's legs all those years ago. Remember that?

BRAD: Pastor, that's *not* what happened! She's the one who started it—

PASTOR: And that was just the Father of Lies speaking through you then! Just like he's speaking through you now! So I am duty bound as your patriarch and spiritual leader to discipline you yet again. You know the drill, Son: hands up for Father God.

BRAD: Pastor, please don't do this, please don't—

PASTOR: Face away from me! *(Pushing Brad)* Hands up for Father God, Brad.

(Brad faces away from Pastor and holds up his hands.)

A REAL MAN

"When I was a child, I spake as a child, I understood as a child, I thought as a child; but when I became a man, I put away childish things."

A REAL MAN DOESN'T HAVE IDLE HANDS
A REAL MAN DOESN'T JACK OFF
A REAL MAN LIVES BY THE MASTER'S COMMANDS
NOT LIKE A PIG SCARFING FROM A TROUGH
A REAL MAN PRACTICES SELF-CONTROL
TO KEEP HIS MORALS ALIGNED
A REAL MAN KEEPS A CLEAN BODY, SOUL,
AND MIND

BRAD: I don't deserve this, Pastor. I was just trying to feel—

(Pastor sadistically whips Brad throughout at unpredictable moments.)

PASTOR:

A REAL MAN TAKES EVERY LASH HE GETS
A REAL MAN HAS A THICK SKIN
A REAL MAN LEARNS FROM ALL HIS REGRETS
SO THAT HE'LL NEVER HAVE THEM AGAIN
A REAL MAN WALKS ON A NARROW PATH
A PATH THE SAVIOR HAS TROD
A REAL MAN MOLDS HIMSELF AFTER FATHER GOD!
I'M WHIPPING YOU, SON, 'CAUSE I LOVE YOU

BRAD: This is love?

PASTOR:

I'M WHIPPING YOU, SON, 'CAUSE I CARE

BRAD: Pastor, please!

PASTOR:

I'M WHIPPING THE HELL OUT OF YOU NOW
TO KEEP YOUR SOUL FROM GOING THERE!

BRAD: I won't do it again!

PASTOR:

DON'T LET SATAN DECEIVE YOU
HE WILL TRY EVERY TRICK
SO KEEP YOUR EYES TURNED TO HEAVEN
AND KEEP YOUR HANDS OFF OF YOUR DICK . . .

(Pastor stands, exhausted from beating Brad, almost as if in a sexual afterglow. Brad lies shaking on the floor.)

It's unclean. And it only leads to pain. For it was the sin of my lusting after your mother that brought you into this world. I thank Father God for bringing Dawn into my life to correct that mistake.

BRAD: Yes, Pastor. I'm sorry I was born, Pastor.

PASTOR *(Attacking Brad with the belt one last time)*: Feeling good is a lie!!!!!

(Pastor takes Brad's VR headset.)

So I'm taking this wickedness out back and I'm gonna burn it. And I better not catch you with another one or your backside is *really* gonna bleed.

BRAD: Yes, Pastor.

PASTOR *(As he exits)*: Amen-amen.

BRAD: Godfather? Truthseekers? Can you hear me? He took my eyes. Can you feel my pain?

(Godfather and the Truthseekers appear in Brad's mind. We only hear their voices.)

TRUTHSEEKER #1: Yeah, Truthseeker. We feel you. But no matter how much Pastor beats up on you, it's Dawn who's the *real* enemy. That's why you've gotta take her down.

TRUTHSEEKER #2: But defeating her won't be easy. Because Pastor is protecting the gash between her legs.

GODFATHER: Because he's a *cuck*, Truthseeker. A zombie slave for the feminocracy. A fate you will share if you don't get up from the floor and stop whimpering like a little *bitch*! Or is that what you are?

BRAD: No!

(Brad slowly stands up.)

A REAL MAN SHAKES OFF HIS FATHER'S LIES
A REAL MAN MAKES HIS OWN WAY
A REAL MAN SEES THE WORLD WITH COLD EYES
IN BLACK AND WHITE
AND IN PREDATOR AND PREY
A REAL MAN TAKES ALL HIS YEARS OF RAGE
THEN HE UNLEASHES THEM MERCILESSLY
'CAUSE IT'S DAWN WHO DESERVES RETRIBUTION
NOT ME

I'm coming like a thief in the night, Sis. And all kinda hell is about to rain down on you.

SCENE FOUR

New Testament Village sanctuary. Tobey is kneeling at the front of the sanctuary, praying. Dawn enters carrying a small gift.

TOBEY: Hi.

DAWN: Hi. I'm ready to unpack if you are. You sounded so serious earlier.

TOBEY: Why don't we sit down?

DAWN: Sure.

(They get chairs and sit down facing one another. Tobey sees Dawn's gift.)

TOBEY: What's that?

DAWN: I brought you a gift.

TOBEY: A gift?

DAWN: I was going to save it for our one-year, but Father God told me I should give it to you now. Open it.

(He opens it. It's a chain with a heart.)

TOBEY: Wow.

DAWN: It's my heart.

TOBEY: Your heart?

DAWN: Yeah. I wanted you to know that you have it.

TOBEY: I can't accept this.

DAWN: Tobey, of course you can. What's wrong? You're scaring me!

TOBEY: Dawn . . . this is what I need to unpack with you. Because as mad as I am at Brock, he's not who I'm really mad at.

DAWN: Who are you mad at?

TOBEY: Myself.

DAWN: Yourself? Why?

TOBEY: Because I'm not pure.

DAWN: What do you mean? Of course you are.

(Silence.)

TOBEY: *No. I've been with a girl before. I'm not a virgin.*

(Silence.)

DAWN: Okay. Who was she?

TOBEY *(Sighs)*: Just this girl I was seeing before my family moved to Eden. And our pastor thought it would be cute to pair us as Joseph and Mary for the Christmas play. And we had written all our own material about how the two of them had this extraordinary love for each other that was tested when Mary got herself pregnant by Father God, and we were rehearsing one night, and one thing led to another, and we were just petting. I didn't even think it was going to go that far. But *that's Satan*. He just *gets right in there*. And I suddenly found my stupid, wicked mouth asking her if I could just put it in for a few seconds, to see how it felt. And she said yes, and then, before I knew it, we were . . . doing it.

DAWN: I see.

TOBEY: You think I'm a pig, don't you?

DAWN: Tobey—

TOBEY: I was going to tell you and Pastor so many times, but then I got scared and told myself that maybe it didn't matter, but then Brock and Amy Sue happened and I realized that the real reason I kept on not telling you is because I've always known that you're too good for me and that if I told you, you would wanna break up with me and—

DAWN: How did it feel inside?

TOBEY: How did what feel inside?

DAWN: The girl you were impure with?

TOBEY: *How did it feel being inside Denise?*

DAWN: Yeah, but we don't need to say her name.

TOBEY: Why are you asking?

DAWN: Because sometimes I wonder what it would be like with us—

TOBEY: With us???

DAWN *(Catching herself)*: On our wedding night if we ever got married.

(Silence.)

TOBEY: You really think about us like that?

DAWN: I do. I do. I know I shouldn't, but I do. Constantly.

TOBEY: It's all I think about too. I have *sooooo* many fantasies . . .

DAWN: You do?

TOBEY: Yeah.

(Silence.)

DAWN: Okay. Um. Well, tell me one.

(Tobey turns away from Dawn.)

PLAYING WITH FIRE

TOBEY:

FIRST, I WOULD TAKE YOUR HAND
THEN, LOVINGLY, I'D EMBRACE YOU
INVITING YOU TO SHARE MY DESIRE
IT WOULDN'T BE SUPER PLANNED
I WOULDN'T WANT TO OUTPACE YOU
'CAUSE THEN I WOULD BE PLAYING WITH FIRE

What do you imagine?

(Nervously, Dawn stands up and faces away from Tobey.)

DAWN:

YOU LAY ME DOWN ON THE BED
THEN, TENDERLY, YOU CARESS ME
INSIDE, I HEAR A HEAVENLY CHOIR
BUT STILL, YOU JUST LIGHTLY TREAD
AND SLOWLY START TO UNDRESS ME
THEN SUDDENLY, WE ARE PLAYING WITH FIRE

TOBEY:

WITH PASSION LIKE WAVES CRASHING INTO
THE SHORE

DAWN:

MY HANDS DOWN YOUR CHEST, DOWN YOUR
BACK, WANTING MORE

TOBEY:

MY LIPS ON YOUR NIPPLES, READY TO EXPLORE
YOUR JUICY INNER ABYSS

DAWN:

I GRAB YOUR FACE AND PULL YOU INTO A KISS
I SPREAD MY LEGS AND PULL YOU INTO MY KISS
YOU SLIP INSIDE ME AND THE WORLD MELTS
INTO BLISS

(They suddenly turn to face each other, eyes open and full of lust.)

TOBEY:

TELL ME I MAKE YOU WET

DAWN:

TOBEY, YOU MAKE ME WET!

TOBEY:

TELL ME YOU WANT TO FUCK ME

DAWN:

IT'S ALL I WANT—

DAWN AND TOBEY:

I WANT YOU TO MAKE ME SQUIRM AND PERSPIRE
THE CLOSER TO YOU I GET
THE HIGHER THIS HIGH-WIRE

(The Promise Keeper Girls appear in Dawn's mind as she approaches Tobey, taking off her jacket, and Tobey approaches Dawn, ripping off his shirt. It is almost as if they are possessed, and in a way, they are—by desire.)

RACHAEL:

YOU BRIM WITH LUST AS YOU'RE PLAYING
WITH FIRE

DAWN:

I WANT YOU BETWEEN MY THIGHS
YOUR COCK IS MY BURIED TREASURE

FIONA AND TRISHA:

YOUR LOINS COMBUST AS YOU'RE PLAYING
WITH FIRE

TOBEY:

I HOPE YOU CAN TAKE THE SIZE
I JUST WANT TO GIVE YOU PLEASURE

PROMISE KEEPER GIRLS:

THERE'S NO SHAME IN PLAYING WITH FIRE
WIN THE GAME CALLED PLAYING WITH FIRE
FEEL THE FLAME OF PLAYING WITH FIRE
PLAYING WITH FIRE, PLAYING WITH FIRE
PLAYING WITH, PLAYING WITH—

(Dawn and Tobey are about to touch when Ryan enters.)

RYAN: Whoops! Okay! Whoa!

(Silence. The spell of desire is broken. The shame quickly sets in.)

TOBEY *(Grabbing his shirt, making a quick exit)*: Oh no. Oh no, oh no, oh no, oh no, oh *no*!!!

DAWN *(Overlapping)*: Tobey! Tobey! Tobey, wait!

RYAN: Tobey, it's okay—

(Tobey exits. Dawn falls to her knees and begins to break.)

Um, Dawn? I'm sorry? I didn't mean to interrupt. I didn't realize anyone was still here, and Tobey sure is fit isn't he . . . oh Dawn, please, please don't be embarrassed?

(Ryan goes to comfort Dawn.)

It's okay. I promise I won't tell anybody? How can I help?

DAWN: I need PKG. Call PKG. Tell them it's an emergency.

RYAN: You got it.

SCENE FIVE

New Testament Village sanctuary. The Promise Keeper Girls enter and sit in a circle around Dawn. Ryan stands outside the circle, observing.

DAWN: It was like I was possessed. I mean, maybe I've had a stray thought here or there, but I've always been able to suppress any feeling of lust that I might have. But this time it was so overpowering. It was like a serpent took over my body, and all I could do was watch from inside myself while it slithered toward Tobey—

RACHAEL *(Explodes)*: STOP MAKING EXCUSES!!

DAWN: I'm not! I swear I'm—

BECKY: *YOU ARE!!!*

DAWN *(Begging)*: Beckyyyyy—

STEPHANIE: DON'T EVEN TRY IT!!!!

DAWN: But you didn't see how Tobey was *looking* at me—

FIONA: NOW YOU'RE BLAMING A *MAN* FOR YOUR WEAKNESS?!?

DAWN: No, I'm just saying that it was bigger than both of—

TRISHA: WHERE WAS YOUR FIG LEAF, WOMAN?!? WHERE WAS YOUR SHAME?!?!?

DAWN: I don't know!

KEKE: DO YOU KNOW HOW MUCH RISK YOU'VE PUT US ALL IN?!?

DAWN: I didn't mean to!

RACHAEL *(Overlapping)*: WHORE!

PROMISE KEEPER GIRLS *(Chanting and pointing, menacingly)*: WHORE!

DAWN: I know I am! I know I am!

(The girls slowly descend upon Dawn.)

PROMISE KEEPER GIRLS *(Overlapping)*: WHORE! WHORE! WHORE! WHORE! WHORE!

RYAN *(As many as he needs to stop PKG)*: STOP! STOP! STOP! STOP! STOP!

RACHAEL: This is none of your business, Ryan! You shouldn't even be here!

RYAN: It *is* my business when I see members of my own church tormenting a fellow sister of the Lord!

STEPHANIE: TORMENTING?!?

KEKE: We're not tormenting! We're holding her *accountable*!!!

BECKY: *Accountable to Father God's holy word!!!*

FIONA: Because "if thy right eye offend thee, pluck it out!!!"

RYAN: Don't you think you're being a little dramatic, Fiona?

TRISHA: Oh who are you to be so high and mighty when I heard that you're nothing but a big fat homo?!?

RYAN: Don't say that word.

STEPHANIE: Is that why your mom won't sit next to you on Sundays?

RYAN: Ummm—

KEKE: So she doesn't even have to *look* at the sissy she gave birth to?

RYAN: It's complica—

RACHAEL: And Fiona, didn't I tell you I thought I saw Ryan drawing Brock Matthews's name into little hearts in his notebook during algebra class?

FIONA: You sure did!

RYAN *(Overlapping)*: Oh God, oh God, oh Godddddd . . .

(Ryan tries to leave, but PKG stops him.)

Please—

TRISHA: Seems like Satan has been hiding a whole lotta secrets in you, sweet cheeks. So what do you have to say about that?

(Stunned silence. Ryan is overwhelmed by shame.)

BORN AGAIN

RYAN *(Spoken)*: IT'S TRUE.

(Sung:)

I'M A GUY WITH A LIFE THAT'S KINDA CHECKERED
I'VE DONE A LOTTA DIRT, AND I'M FAR FROM
SQUEAKY CLEAN
THOUGH I'VE TRIED TO ERASE ALL THE BLACK
MARKS FROM MY RECORD
TO SOME, I'M STILL KNOWN AS THE CREAMPIE
ANAL QUEEN!

(PKG gasps in collective horror.)

I JUST CAN'T RESIST GETTING NAKED WITH THE CAM'RAS ROLLING
AND POSTING MY ASS FOR STRANGERS ON THE INTERNET
THEN SETTING UP DATES FOR THE PURPOSE OF CORNHOLING
BUT ONCE IT'S ALL DONE, ALL I FEEL IS DEEP REGRET
I'VE HARBORED THESE DESIRES SINCE ONLY LORD KNOWS WHEN
BUT CAN'T I BE FORGIVEN, REGARDLESS OF HOW WICKED I'VE BEEN?
AND BE BORN AGAIN!
AND BE BORN AGAIN!
I WON'T MAKE PORN AGAIN!
WHEN I'M BORN AGAIN!

(He goes to Dawn.)

WE ALL DESERVE A SECOND CHANCE
A SPIRITUAL REBIRTH
A CHANCE TO TURN OUR LIVES AROUND AND BUILD BACK UP OUR WORTH
CAN'T WE BE BORN AGAIN?

Purity is important, and I've definitely failed there, but what about *JESUS*? *Redemption? Resurr—*

TRISHA: UH-UH! No cross, no crown, Ryan! Salvation is earned! It's NOT a "get out of jail free" card!!!!

RYAN: Maybe it's not, Trisha, but what if I happened to hack into any one of your internet search histories? What if I already have? Think about that and then tell me who here *isn't* without some sort of sexual sin?

BECKY *(Spoken)*: IT'S TRUE!

(Sung:)

I ONCE SELF-ABUSED WITH A ZUCCHINI

KEKE:

SOMETIMES WHEN PASTOR PREACHES, I TOUCH MYSELF BELOW

STEPHANIE:

ONE NIGHT I WAS BAD AND I STROKED MY DOGGY'S WEENIE

FIONA AND RACHAEL:

I'VE DONE MUCH WORSE—TRUST ME YOU DON'T WANT TO KNOW

TRISHA:

I'M REALLY INTO PICTURES OF DECAPITATED NAKED MEN

PROMISE KEEPER GIRLS *(Caught off guard by this particular perversion)*: Whoa!

DAWN:

AND JOHN 3 AND 3 SAYS WE ONLY GET TO PARADISE WHEN
WE ARE BORN AGAIN!

RYAN:

WHEN WE'RE BORN AGAIN!

DAWN:

NEVER MOURN AGAIN!

RYAN:

WHEN YOU'RE BORN AGAIN!
IF WE JUST ASK TO BE REDEEMED
THEN HE'LL FORGIVE THE PAST

DAWN:

HE'LL WRAP US IN HIS LOVING ARMS
HIS MERCY IS SO VAST

RYAN:

FILL UP WITH HIS GLORY

DAWN:

YEAH!

RYAN:

DROWN IN JESUS'S BLOOD

DAWN:

OOH!

RYAN:

BATHE IN FULL REPENTANCE LIKE PIGS BATHE IN THE MUD

PROMISE KEEPER GIRLS:

AH, BORN AGAIN!

DAWN:

STRIP YOURSELF TO NOTHING!

RYAN:

NOTHING!

DAWN:

GET UP ON THE CROSS!

RYAN:

JESUS!

DAWN:

WALK TO YOUR GOLGOTHA AND BURN AWAY
THE DROSS

PROMISE KEEPER GIRLS:

BORN AGAIN!

RYAN:

DUNK ME IN THE WATER
WASH AWAY MY SHAME
PAIR ME WITH THE GIRL WHO WILL PROUDLY
TAKE MY NAME

PROMISE KEEPER GIRLS:

BORN AGAIN!

RYAN:

PRESS OUR FLESH TOGETHER
BLESS ME AS HER GROOM
WATCH ME BE REBORN AS I FERTILIZE HER WOMB

RYAN:	PROMISE KEEPER GIRLS:
'CAUSE I'M SICK OF ALWAYS FEELING	AH
LIKE I'M JUST AN ALSO-RAN	
AND I'M SICK OF ALWAYS FEELING	AH
LIKE I'M REALLY NOT A MAN	
LORD, I'M SICK OF ALWAYS FEELING	AH
LIKE A TOTAL LESSER-THAN	
I JUST WANT TO BE NORMAL	

DAWN:

I KNOW THAT YOU CAN!

RYAN:

I CAN?

DAWN:

YOU CAN!

RYAN:

I CAN!

DAWN:

YOU CAN!

RYAN:

I CAN I CAN I CAN I CAN I CAN I CAN
BE BORN AGAIN!

PROMISE KEEPER GIRLS:

CAN CAN CAN AH . . . BORN AGAIN!

RYAN:

WE'LL BE BORN AGAIN!

DAWN:

WE'LL NEVER MOURN AGAIN!

PROMISE KEEPER GIRLS:

BORN AGAIN!

RYAN:

WHEN WE'RE BORN AGAIN!

PROMISE KEEPER GIRLS:

BORN AGAIN!

<table>
<tr><td>RYAN:</td><td>PROMISE KEEPER GIRLS:</td></tr>
<tr><td>OUR DESTINIES WILL BE
REVERSED</td><td>AH</td></tr>
<tr><td>WITH JESUS BY OUR SIDE</td><td></td></tr>
<tr><td>IN WORD AND WATER BE
IMMERSED</td><td>AH</td></tr>
<tr><td>AND BE TRANSMOGRIFIED!</td><td></td></tr>
<tr><td>AND BE BORN AGAIN!</td><td></td></tr>
</table>

PROMISE KEEPER GIRLS:

AGAIN! AGAIN!

DAWN:

AGAIN!

PROMISE KEEPER GIRLS:

AGAIN! AGAIN!

RYAN:

AGAIN!

PROMISE KEEPER GIRLS:

OH!

DAWN:

AGAIN!

PROMISE KEEPER GIRLS:

OH!

RYAN:

AGAIN!

PROMISE KEEPER GIRLS:

OH!

DAWN:

AGAIN!

PROMISE KEEPER GIRLS:

OH!

RYAN:

AGAIN!

PROMISE KEEPER GIRLS:

OH!

DAWN:

AGAIN!

ALL:

AGAIN!

(Dawn, Ryan and PKG huddle up and celebrate.)

TRISHA: I'm sorry, y'all. I was in such denial about my own perversions that I lost myself for a second.

RACHAEL: Me too.

KEKE, STEPHANIE, FIONA AND BECKY: Me three.

DAWN: It's okay. It's okay. But I think we all really need to thank *you*, Ryan. Without your testimony, we never could have gotten here.

(PKG agrees in a verbal jumble.)

RYAN: No! It's because of YOU guys that I get to start over with Father God? You'll see! I'm gonna leave this gay crap *totally* behind and be a real man finally?

(Dawn and PKG cheer on Ryan.)

FIONA: So now what? Confessing our sexual sins to each other is one thing, but the scripture says we can't enter the kingdom of Heaven until we're *actually* born of the water and the spirit.

STEPHANIE: Well, we've got the water right here in the baptismal pool.

RACHAEL: But what about the spirit? Only *Pastor* can direct the flow of the spirit.

KEKE: Why don't we call Pastor right now and ask him to come here and rebaptize us?!?

BECKY: Let's call everybody who wants or needs to be rebaptized! Even Brock and Amy Sue!

TRISHA: It'll be like a late-night spring revival!

(PKG laughs.)

DAWN: Everybody hang on. It's been a long, emotional night and I think we need to get some sleep so that we're clear-headed when we talk to Pastor first thing tomorrow morning, okay? Let's say nine-ish?

KEKE: Ahhhh! I'm so excited!

(The rest of PKG joins in Keke's excitement as they exit. Ryan goes to Dawn.)

RYAN: Hey, Dawn?

DAWN: What's up?

RYAN: This is completely life-changing for me and I'm so geeked about straightening my walk with Father God, but I'm also clear on the fact that I am like, the biggest sissy in the entire world, so you don't think I'm kidding myself, do you?

DAWN: First of all, no you're not. And second of all, was the apostle Paul kidding himself when he said, "All things work together to them that love God—"

RYAN *(Finishing the scripture she's quoting)*: "—and to them who are called according to His purpose." You're right, you're right. So how about we blow this joint? It's pretty late. Do you want me to walk you home?

DAWN: No, I'll be okay. And there's something really important that I need to take care of before I get home anyway.

RYAN: Cool beans. See you in the morning.

SCENE SIX

Nighttime. Tobey waits at the lake. A distant banshee cry interrupts the calm. He looks around but sees nothing. The Promise Keeper Girls enter in a processional as figments of Dawn, who follows behind.

WHEN SHE GAVE BIRTH

PROMISE KEEPER GIRLS:

WHEN SHE GAVE BIRTH TO SIN AND SHAME
TWO SERPENTS CRAWLED UPON THE EARTH
THEY ASKED, "WHAT IS OUR FATHER'S NAME?"
SHE WEPT AND CLAIMED A VIRGIN BIRTH

DAWN: Hi.
TOBEY: Hi.
DAWN: I wasn't sure you would come.

TOBEY: I wasn't sure I should after what happened, but I also wanted to tell you in person how sorry I am for my immodesty and for compromising—

DAWN: No. *I* shouldn't have created the opportunity for temptation when I asked you such compromising questions about Denise!

TOBEY: Temptation or not, I'm the man and I should have stopped it! It was all me! You're perfect!

DAWN: Stop saying I'm perfect! I'm not perfect, you're not perfect. We're black with sin. We were born with it. There's no getting around it.

(Tobey groans with shame.)

Tobey, no! What I'm trying to say is we're not alone! Everybody is struggling with the same sexual demons! Which is why we have to battle those demons as a community.

TOBEY: A community?

DAWN: Yes. Tomorrow morning we're going to Pastor together to ask him to rebaptize us. All of PKG, Ryan, we're even going to call Brock and Amy Sue. And I want you beside me. So no more breakup talk.

(She takes his hand—it's electric.)

I love you and I'm never letting you go. Ever.

TOBEY: Love me? How could you love me?

(He starts to break down.)

DAWN: Tobey, what's wrong?

TOBEY: Everything you're saying feels so good, but tomorrow's too late for me, Dawn. There's something that's so ugly and dark and satanic clattering inside of me and—

DAWN: No, it's never too late to start over! Think of how clean we'll be!

TOBEY: How clean we'll be? Clean? Clean . . . Yes. Maybe we really can be clean if you come in the lake with me?

DAWN: The lake? What?

TOBEY: I know it sounds so crazy, but let's baptize each other NOW so we can wash all of this sin and confusion away NOW!

DAWN: Tobe—

TOBEY: I'm *scared*, Dawn! I've never been more terrified in my life! I never fully atoned for what I did with Denise, and I think that's why I messed up with you and why I'll keep messing up unless I deal with this now! Please. PLEASE.

(Silence.)

DAWN: Okay. Okay, yes. If that's what you need us to do.

TOBEY: It is.

DAWN: Okay. Then let's do it.

(Dawn and Tobey take off their shoes and wade into the lake.)

PROMISE KEEPER GIRLS:

WHEN SHE GAVE BIRTH TO SIN AND SHAME

TOBEY *(Spoken)*:

Let's hold up our hands. In the Old Testament, we learn that Original Sin was born from Mother Eve when she allowed herself to be beguiled by the serpent.

PROMISE KEEPER GIRLS:

TWO SERPENTS
CRAWLED
UPON
THE EARTH

DAWN *(Spoken)*:

I hold up my hands, God,
I hold up my hands.

PROMISE KEEPER GIRLS:

THEY ASKED,
"WHAT IS OUR
FATHER'S
NAME?"

TOBEY:

And she tempted Adam, the first man, with fruit from the Tree of Knowledge—the *very* tree the Lord God had commanded them not to eat.

SHE WEPT AND
CLAIMED A
VIRGIN BIRTH

DAWN:

I hold up my hands, God,
I hold up my hands.

SHE WEPT AND
CLAIMED A
VIRGIN BIRTH

TOBEY: And for their disobedience, sin entered the world, and they were turned out of paradise forever.

DAWN: But the *New* Testament tells us that we must be born again. Of water and of the spirit. So I, Dawn Elizabeth O'Keefe, do solemnly swear to go forward and sin no more.

TOBEY: And I, Tobey Zacharias Akin, do solemnly vow to go forward and sin no more. With this water, we do now purify. On the count of three. One . . . Two . . . Three . . .

(During the following, Tobey and Dawn baptize each other.)

PROMISE KEEPER GIRLS:

WHEN SHE GAVE BIRTH TO SIN AND SHAME
TWO SERPENTS CRAWLED UPON THE EARTH
THEY ASKED, "WHAT IS OUR FATHER'S NAME?"
SHE WEPT AND CLAIMED A VIRGIN BIRTH

DAWN:	PROMISE KEEPER GIRLS:
Wow.	SHE WEPT AND
TOBEY:	
I feel so clean.	CLAIMED A
DAWN:	
Jesus is so precious!	VIRGIN BIRTH
TOBEY:	
Do you see what I mean now?	SHE WEPT AND
DAWN:	
Yes. This was such a good idea.	CLAIMED A
TOBEY:	
I don't want to lose this, Dawn.	VIRGIN
DAWN:	
Me neither.	BIRTH

TOBEY: So marry me.

DAWN: Marry you?

TOBEY: Yes. Become my wife, my helpmeet, my partner for life.

DAWN: You're serious.

TOBEY: I am. Tomorrow when we go to Pastor, we can tell him and NTV that we've been born again, together forever.

DAWN: But we're still in school! And what will your parents say? And Tobey . . . I don't know what kind of wife I could be to you because . . . I have so much shame in my body. *So* much shame—

TOBEY: Dawn, you don't think I have shame in my body *too*?

(PKG hums.)

But the shame is kind of a blessing. I think Father God puts shame in us to protect us until we find our helpmeets, who help us become who we're meant to be.

DAWN: You really think so?

TOBEY: I know so. But there can't be any daylight between us on this, Dawn, or it won't work. I care about *you*. I love *you*, I want *you*. Please marry me.

(Silence.)

DAWN: Yes.

TOBEY: YES! My wife! My wife!

DAWN: Your wife! Your wife!

(Tobey takes Dawn into his arms and they kiss. Desire returns.)

TOBEY: Our first kiss!

DAWN: Our first kiss!

(Silence. They kiss again, more passionately. Then Tobey places his hand over Dawn's heart.)

TOBEY: Therefore shall a man leave his father and his mother, and shall cleave unto his wife: and they shall be one flesh. *Husband. Wife.*

DAWN: *Husband. Wife.*

TOBEY *(Gently)*: Take off your promise ring.

DAWN: Now?

TOBEY: One flesh, Dawn. But only if you—

DAWN: No, I do. I do.

(Dawn removes the ring.)

TOBEY: Hearing you say "I do" is like music to my ears. So let's sing.

(Tobey positions Dawn between himself and a rock.)

DAWN: It's kind of cold all of a sudden. Are you cold?
TOBEY: No.

(He kisses and touches Dawn all over. She squirms.)

DAWN: Now something's poking me in the back.
TOBEY: Shhh . . .
DAWN: Sorry.
TOBEY: I'm removing the barriers between us now, okay?

(He slips off Dawn's underwear and discards it.)

DAWN: Now I'm really cold.
TOBEY: "Husbands, love your wives as Christ loved the church." That's all I want to do, Wife.
DAWN: That's all I want too, but—
TOBEY: Listen to the wind rustling through the trees. Look at the stars. Feel the warmth between us.

(Tobey backs Dawn into the rock, pinning her arms up.)

DAWN: Hey Tobey, maybe we could—
TOBEY: Father God is smiling down us.
DAWN: What if we just—
TOBEY: The way He smiled on Solomon and his beloved.
DAWN *(Trying to spot her discarded underwear)*: Um, where did you put my—
TOBEY: What a blessing you are to me! What a precious gift!

(He begins to penetrate her. She begins to moan in discomfort.)

DAWN *(Spoken)*:
Precious gift.
Precious gift.
Precious gift.
Precious gift.

PROMISE KEEPER GIRLS:
WHEN SHE
GAVE BIRTH
TO SIN AND
SHAME

TOBEY *(Overlapping)*: Breathe into me, Wife. Breathe into me. Breathe into me—YES—

DAWN *(Overlapping)*:
Tobey, I have a cramp—

PROMISE KEEPER GIRLS:
TWO
SERPENTS
CRAWLED
UPON THE
EARTH

TOBEY *(Ignoring her, overlapping)*: Feel me, Dawn. Merge with me and let my love envelop and edify you and—sweet Father Godddd—

DAWN *(Overlapping)*:
I can't feel my legs—

PROMISE KEEPER GIRLS:
THEY ASKED,
"WHAT IS
OUR FATHER'S
NAME?"

TOBEY *(Ignoring her, overlapping)*: And it came to pass that Tobey saw there a daughter of Eden whose name was Dawn . . .

DAWN *(Overlapping)*:
I feel like I'm gonna
pass out—

PROMISE KEEPER GIRLS:
SHE WEPT AND
CLAIMED
A VIRGIN
BIRTH

TOBEY *(Ignoring her, overlapping)*: . . . whose purity was unmatched, and whose hair was the glory of all of Corinthians . . .

DAWN *(Overlapping)*:
Why can't I feel my legs—

PROMISE KEEPER GIRLS:
SHE WEPT AND
CLAIMED
A VIRGIN
BIRTH

TOBEY *(Ignoring her, overlapping)*: . . . and she gazed upon her betrothed with a desire consecrated by Father God . . .

DAWN *(Overlapping)*:
Tobey, please, please—

PROMISE KEEPER GIRLS:
SHE WEPT AND
CLAIMED
A VIRGIN
BIRTH

TOBEY *(Ignoring her, overlapping)*: *He took her and went in unto her and he took her and . . .*

DAWN *(Overlapping)*:
Tobey, stop—

PROMISE KEEPER GIRLS:
SHE WEPT AND
CLAIMED

TOBEY *(Ignoring her, overlapping)*: *. . . he went in unto her and he took her and went in unto her and . . .*

(Another banshee cry. This time it's loud and present. An unholy light fills the air.)

DAWN *(Overlapping)*:
TOBEY, YOU'RE
HURTING—

PROMISE KEEPER GIRLS:
A VIRGIN—

(Dawn's vaginal teeth chomp down on Tobey. As Tobey pulls away, blood pumps from between his legs. His penis is gone.)

TOBEY: AHHHHHHHHHHHHHH!!!!!!!!!!!!!!!!!

(Tobey falls into the lake. Dawn grabs her clothes and flees in fear. PKG exits, the unholy light disappearing with them. Brad emerges from his hiding place.)

BRAD: The fall of man is upon us. The fall of man is upon us! Unholy fucking Jesus! THE FALL OF MAN IS UPON US!!!!

(Blackout.)

SCENE SEVEN

The Promise Keeper Girls text each other as they head to NTV.

KEKE: So I don't know what this means, but I had the weirdest dream last night?

RACHAEL: Me too. Mine had this woman in it? Or at least I *think* she was a woman?

FIONA: She was clothed in red. Or was it blood? And I know I've never seen her before, but why did she feel so familiar to me?

BECKY: I feel like she said she'd been imprisoned for centuries but now she was free?

STEPHANIE: And something about her host body almost being ready?

TRISHA: And something about being born again through her whether we liked it or not?

KEKE: Wait! Where's Dawn? Has anybody heard from Dawn?

(Ryan enters on his phone.)

RYAN: Dawn, is everything okay? I thought we were all going to meet with Pastor at NTV this morning and be born again?
BECKY: Does the weather seem kinda off to you guys, or is it just me?
RYAN: Dawn, I'm back at home and just heard the news on my police scanner. *Please* call me.
RACHAEL: Why does my head hurt?
FIONA: Why does my stomach hurt?
TRISHA: Why does my whole body hurt?
RYAN: Dawn, what's going on?
BECKY: What's happening to us?
RACHAEL AND STEPHANIE: Maybe it's dark-sided.
RYAN: What's happened to you, Dawn?
PROMISE KEEPER GIRLS: Maybe it's dark-sided!

(Pastor barges into New Testament Village with PKG. We segue into . . .)

SCENE EIGHT

Pastor is completely frantic.

PASTOR: Promise Keeper Girls! Please tell me you've seen Dawn?

FIONA: No! What happened?!?

PASTOR: Her bed wasn't slept in! She's not answering any of my calls! I don't think she's heard the news!

STEPHANIE: What news?

PASTOR: He's dead! I felt him die in my dreams, PKG!

BECKY: *Who's* dead, Pastor?!?

PASTOR: Tobey!

(The Promise Keeper Girls gasp.)

They found his body floating in Lake Eden! He was naked! The meat of Adam torn from between his legs and cast aside like a piece of spoiled pork loin!

PROMISE KEEPER GIRLS: Oh no!

PASTOR: When I awakened from slumber, Father God told me that Dawn is in grave danger and that Tobey's death was the beginning of the end! The time has come, PKG! The beast has risen!

PROMISE KEEPER GIRLS: The beast?!?

TRISHA: But Pastor, you don't mean—

PASTOR: The serpent! The *dragon*! To safeguard you angels from the beast, you must remain locked in this sanctuary until I return with your sister, Dawn!

(Pastor exits in a rush. PKG gathers, shell-shocked.)

TEETH

FIONA:

I'M REALLY SCARED
ARE WE IN THE BOOK OF REVELATION?
AND IF SO, THEN WHAT'S NEXT?
WHAT'S LYING AHEAD?

(Elsewhere on stage we see Pastor running through Eden, looking for Dawn.)

PASTOR: Dawn, can you hear me?!?

KEKE:

WE'RE NOT PREPARED
WE NEED MORE THAN JUST THIS CONGREGATION
BECKY, LOOK AT THE SKY
IT'S TURNING BLOOD RED!

PASTOR: I'm your protector!!

BECKY:

IF THIS IS HOW THE WORLD ENDS
I'M IN GOOD COMPANY
IF I HAVE TO DIE, I'LL DIE WITH PKG!

PASTOR: I'll *KILL* to protect your purity!!!!

RACHAEL:

I'M NOT OKAY
THIS WHOLE THING FEELS REALLY EERIE
THE HAIR ON MY ARM IS STANDING ON END

PASTOR: Resist the serpent!

STEPHANIE:

LET'S RUN AWAY
'CAUSE IF I'M CORRECT IN MY THEORY
THEN THE BEAST COULD BE CLOSE
ABOUT TO DESCEND

(Trisha feels a sharp cramp.)

TRISHA:

I THINK SHE'S ALREADY HERE!

(The rest of PKG feels sharp cramps.)

THERE'S NOWHERE WE CAN HIDE
SHE'S TAKING CONTROL OF ME FROM INSIDE!

(All at once, their vaginal teeth emerge. SHING!)

PROMISE KEEPER GIRLS:

THERE IS A DARK, SATANIC COLLISION
RISING FROM UNDERNEATH

(They reach into their underwear.)

SOMETHING THAT HUNTS WITH LASER
PRECISION

(They pull out their hands to reveal their fingertips smeared with menstrual blood.)

TEETH, TEETH, TEETH, TEETH

(They flick the blood from their hands, splattering the space around them.)

I CLOSE MY EYES AND I CAN ENVISION
TEETH, TEETH, TEETH, TEETH

TEETH, TEETH, TEETH, TEETH

(Pastor rings the plague bell.)

PASTOR: People of Eden! We must vanquish the Antichrist! His sharp fangs drip with the meat of Adam and the blood of Eve! The beast approaches! The beast approaches!

(Brad enters and emphatically calls out to Godfather.)

BRAD: Godfather! Are you there? I witnessed my stepsister Dawn exercising the ultimate power of the feminocracy between her thighs, and now the fate of mankind literally *hangs* in the balance! Oh, Godfather, please hear me!!! This is far worse than we could have imagined!

BRAD AND PASTOR:

DARK MOONS ARE RISING, WET WITH DEPRAVITY!

(The Truthseekers appear. They feel the pain in their index fingers calling them to action.)

TRUTHSEEKERS:

DARK MOONS ARE RISING!

BRAD AND PASTOR:

RISING FROM UNDERNEATH!

TRUTHSEEKERS:

FROM UNDERNEATH!

BRAD AND PASTOR:

OUT OF THE SWAMP OF EACH VAGINAL CAVITY

ALL:

TEETH, TEETH, TEETH, TEETH!
UNDER THE EARTH, I CAN HEAR ALL THIS
CLATTERING
IT'S RISING FROM UNDERNEATH

BRAD:

BETWEEN THEIR LEGS, A SET OF SHARP
CHATTERING

ALL:

TEETH, TEETH, TEETH, TEETH
TEETH, TEETH, TEETH, TEETH . . .

(PKG growls as they exit.)

GODFATHER: The feminocracy will fall, Truthseeker, and Dawn with it. But only if you do *exactly* as I command.

BRAD: I'll do whatever you say to stop the fall of mankind, Godfather.

(He runs off.)

SCENE NINE

Dawn's bedroom. Ryan sits with Dawn, trying to keep her calm.

DAWN: So then I stopped him. Or it stopped him. I don't even know how to explain it. It happened so fast: one minute he was inside of me, and the next he was screaming and drowning in the water, and it's all because I—

RYAN: Dawn, no. Look at me. Look at me. You didn't do anything wrong? You're perfect—

DAWN: If I'm so perfect, then why did I hide outside my house all night? Why did I wait until I knew Pastor and Brad weren't home before I came back this morning?!?

RYAN: Why *wouldn't* you hide after going through something that traumatic? Listen, I don't want to put words in your mouth, but Dawn, it sounds like . . . like Tobey *raped you.*

DAWN: Okay. Yes. But even if that's true, what about what I did to him down there?

RYAN: That was just your eyes playing tricks on you—

DAWN: Ryan, I literally pulled it out of me and threw it into the lake!

(Silence.)

RYAN: Okay, I'm stumped on that one.

DAWN: See?!?

RYAN: No. I think we just need to get you to a doctor and get you checked out.

DAWN: What?

RYAN: There's a doctor I heard about who's got a clinic just outside of Eden, and I think his name is Dr. Godfrey—

DAWN: No. No doctors. Now that I'm here, I have to face the consequences for what I did to Tobey. I have to answer to Father God for my sin.

RYAN: You're not the one who sinned here, Dawn. And even if you had, Father God loves us despite our sins.

DAWN: And sometimes you have to punish those you love to teach them. It's what I deserve. So I appreciate you dropping by, but Father God and I need to talk before Pastor comes home.

RYAN: Okay. But call me if you change your mind about Dr. Godfrey.

(Ryan exits. Dawn begins to pray to Father God.)

ALWAYS THE WOMAN

DAWN:

THE DEVIL CALLED ME DOWN TO THE LAKE
I THOUGHT THAT HE WAS YOU
BUT I MADE A MISTAKE

I WAS TOO EAGER AND COULD NOT SEE
THE TRAP THAT HE HAD LAIN FOR ME
BUT THAT'S A COP-OUT—I PLAYED MY PART
BY TEMPTING TOBEY WITH THE PROMISE OF
MY HEART

(Dawn finds the chain she had given to Tobey.)

HOW LONG HAVE I HAD THIS BLIND SPOT?
IT WAS SO SIMPLE, STILL I FORGOT . . .

IT'S ALWAYS THE WOMAN
THE DEVIL WILL CLAIM
IT'S ALWAYS THE WOMAN
HER BIRTHRIGHT IS SHAME
HER BODY'S DESIRE
THE CAUSE OF HER CHASTENING
THE GENESIS OF, THE GENESIS OF
ALL SUFFERING

(The Promise Keeper Girls appear in Dawn's mind.)

TRISHA: Since the beginning.
STEPHANIE: It's in your DNA.
KEKE: Your *mother's* DNA.
RACHAEL: Your mother passed her wantonness down to you as hers did to her.
BECKY: Inherited like a curse, from mother to daughter and to all mankind.
FIONA: The root of all evil. The *fruit* of all evil. In your body.
PROMISE KEEPER GIRLS: *Your* body.

DAWN:

THE SERPENT SLITHERED DOWN THROUGH
THE YEARS
I DIDN'T HEAR HIS SUBTLE HISSING IN MY EARS
THOUGH I LOVED TOBEY, I BELIEVE
I CAUSED HIS DOWNFALL
I'M JUST LIKE EVE
AND JUST LIKE EVE, MY BODY'S BEEN CURSED
AND I DON'T KNOW IF IT CAN BE REVERSED
AND THE SERPENT WEARS A NEW DISGUISE
HE'S CLOTHED IN FLESH BETWEEN MY THIGHS

'CAUSE IT'S ALWAYS THE WOMAN
THE SERPENT DISTRACTS
IT'S ALWAYS THE WOMAN
THE SERPENT ATTRACTS

DAWN:	PROMISE KEEPER GIRLS:
THAT'S WHY I AM CURSED	AH
WHY I AM CURSED	AH
I ATE THE FRUIT	AH, AH
I WASN'T COERCED	AH
I DISOBEYED	AH
I DISOBEYED	AH, AH
I BEG YOU, FATHER GOD	
I'M SO AFRAID	AH, AH
DON'T DESERT ME	AH, AH
PLEASE LET ME ATONE	OOH
BUT IF YOU CAN'T FORGIVE ME	OOH
IF YOU JUST CAN'T HEAL ME	

DAWN:

I PRAY THAT YOU WON'T LEAVE ME ALONE

(Brad enters.)

BRAD: You're under arrest!

(Dawn jumps, screaming in surprise. Brad laughs.)

I got you.

DAWN: I don't have time for your sick games, Brad. I need to talk to Pastor.

BRAD: About what? About how gruesome and sexy Tobey's murder was?

DAWN: Brad, please go.

BRAD: Father God sure punishes in mysterious ways, doesn't He?

DAWN: Brad, PLEASE.

BRAD: No, I can't leave you like this, Dawn. Not now. And besides, you're always "checking in" on me so now I'm "checking in" on you, so *how's your heart*?

DAWN: Broken.

BRAD: Aww, poor thing. I haven't seen you this sad since your mom died.

(Dawn tries to leave.)

DAWN: You don't get to talk about my mom anymore. I'll wait for Pastor outside on the porch.

BRAD: Have you ever thought about how Kim died? Lady cancer? Isn't that what Pastor called it?

(Dawn stops, her curiosity piqued.)

DAWN: Yeah? Because that's what it was.

BRAD: Kind of unscientific sounding, don't you think?

DAWN *(More defensive than she'd like to be)*: No, not really. What do you mean? I dunno. We were so little that I never thought about . . . I mean, I guess I always assumed it had something to do with . . .

BRAD: With her snatch?

DAWN: Don't call it that!

BRAD: Pastor never fucked her, you know.

DAWN: What?

BRAD: Maybe he never told you, but he told me a couple of beatings ago.

DAWN: He never said that.

BRAD: Apparently she wanted it, even right up until the end when the cancer had spread to her cooch, but he refused to stick it in—

DAWN: Stop it! You're disgusting.

BRAD: Anyway, it came to mind since I saw you sawing off Tobey's wiener with your precious gift down at Lake Eden last night.

(This stops Dawn dead in her tracks.)

DAWN: You saw me and Tobey?

BRAD: Oh yeah. I was there. I saw everything.

DAWN: *Oh no, oh no, oh noooooo . . .*

BRAD *(Overlapping)*: So you should probably get yourself checked out before you fuck-marry-kill again.

(He laughs at his own joke.)

DAWN *(Desperate)*: Brad, you have to help me!

BRAD: Do you *admit* what you did to me when we were kids now?!?

DAWN *(Overlapping)*: I swear I don't remember! Please help me!

BRAD *(Overlapping)*: Shut up, shut up! Yes, you do, and I'm not lifting a finger to—

DAWN *(Overlapping)*: But we're family! We're family!

BRAD: The hell we are! There's *nothing* between us! And now it's *your* turn to suffer! And with Godfather's help, my brothers and I are gonna make sure you and your coven get what's coming to you!

(Brad grabs Dawn in a fit of rage. Pastor enters, having heard the shouting. He's in an anxious state.)

PASTOR: Dawn?!? Baby?!?

DAWN: Pastor, I—

PASTOR: BRAD, WHAT ARE YOU DOING?!? GET YOUR HANDS OFF DAWN NOW!!!

BRAD *(Overlapping)*: You come at me again and I'll knock your head off!

DAWN: BRAD, NO!

PASTOR: DAWN, did he hurt you?!?

DAWN: PASTOR, I'M OKAY! I need to talk about Tobey—

BRAD *(Overlapping)*: YOU'RE TAKING HER SIDE AGAIN!!! Because you're in on it! *That's* why you've been protecting her all these years!

PASTOR *(Overlapping)*: To Hell with you, demon spawn. Go join your mother in the lake of fire! *(To Dawn, urgent)* Baby, listen to me, I wanted to be the one to tell you about Tobey, but we're almost out of time and I need you to come to NTV with me *right now* because Father God has been speaking to me and sending me visions— *(To Brad)* SHUTUPSHUTUPSHUTUP!!!!

DAWN: Visions?!? Visions of what?!?

BRAD *(Overlapping)*: Hey Dawn, did you ever wonder why Pastor can't keep a woman in his house without her running out on him or dying of lady cancer or sprouting a dragon pussy like you? It's because he's a cuck for the feminocracy! He's a cuck for the motherfucking feminocracy!

(Brad laughs maniacally at the truth he believes he's found.)

PASTOR *(Continuous)*: . . . and He told me that what happened to Tobey was not natural and that the beast is loose in Eden and that it's time for Father God's soldiers to suit up for the unholy war!

BRAD *(Overlapping)*: Oh my God! Oh my *fucking* God! He's insane! He's insane!

DAWN: The unholy war?!?

PASTOR: Yes, the unholy war!

BRAD *(Using his hands as a megaphone)*: It's probably a ploy to get in your pants, Dawn! I hope you can see that!

PASTOR: WHAT DID YOU JUST SAY?!?

BRAD: I said it's probably a ploy so you can finally split your little girl's beaver—

PASTOR: Demon!

BRAD *(Continuous)*: . . . which you've probably been dreaming about since you first laid eyes on her—

(Pastor attacks.)

PASTOR: Get the hell out of my house, demon!

(Brad fights back.)

BRAD: You cuck bastard!

DAWN: Brad, stop!

PASTOR: SHUT YOUR MOUTH!

BRAD: That's how sick you are! You actually *want* her to chew your dick off like she chewed off Tobey's, don't you?

(Pastor prevails. He knocks Brad to the floor and pulls a knife on him.)

PASTOR: The Father of Lies might speak through you, but the hand of Father God is undefeated! I cast thee out, demon! I cast thee out! There's no place for you here!

BRAD: I meant what I said, Dawn. Me and my brothers are comin' for you.

PASTOR: OUT!

(Brad exits. Pastor puts his knife away.)

It's okay now. He can't hurt you anymore. I won't let anybody hurt you. Father God is using me as a sword and a shield to protect you from the red dragon that—

DAWN: Pastor, is it true that you never consummated your marriage to my mom?

PASTOR: I don't want to talk about that! Why are you asking me about that—

DAWN: Pastor—

PASTOR: There's no time to entertain the lies that demon spreads, because the beast—

DAWN: But is it true, Pastor? Is it true you never consummated?

PASTOR: Of course it's true! Kim's body was cursed with lady cancer from being a loose woman before we got married.

DAWN: How do you know?

PASTOR: Father God told me, now let's g—

DAWN: But she was never in treatment, right? I don't think I remember any doctors or anything.

PASTOR *(Exasperated)*: She had the greatest doctor this world has ever known, baby! *Jehovah! Father God! The Great "I Am"!* And His prescription was that we fast and pray! And yes, Kim wanted me to lie with her because she thought the meat of Adam might heal her, but I was afraid it wasn't clean enough, and Father God told me to gird my loins because His judgment would soon be upon her. And so it was. And she died. That was her punishment.

DAWN: But if lady cancer and death were Father God's punishment to Mom for being a loose woman, what was I?

PASTOR: A precious gift, Dawn.

DAWN: But how do you know it isn't like, genetic or something?

PASTOR: Baby, if you had inherited lady cancer from Kim, I would have slain you with a dagger even sharper than this one before Father God Himself. But Father God had higher plans for you. He said I should start you on the path to purity with PKG. That's why tonight, we crusade! Because we have been anointed by Father God to avenge Tobey and vanquish the Antichrist once and for all! Amen-amen!

DAWN *(Fearfully humoring him)*: Amen-amen! But Pastor, we can't battle the Antichrist in these filthy civilian clothes. We must cleanse ourselves, and only *then* will we be prepared to fight the red dragon!

PASTOR: Yes, of course! Leviticus and Revelation! How could I have forgotten the scriptures?

(Pastor rushes for the door and exits.)

SHAME IN MY BODY (REPRISE)

DAWN:

I'VE GOTTA FIX WHAT'S WRONG WITH MY BODY
'CAUSE PASTOR IS SICK IN THE HEAD
AND I'VE GOTTA FIX WHAT'S WRONG WITH
MY BODY
'CAUSE IF I GO WITH PASTOR INSTEAD
I'M GOOD AS DEAD . . .

(She grabs items she needs to make a quick escape and exits.)

SCENE TEN

Dawn waits in an examination room. Dr. Godfrey enters, looking at an intake form on a clipboard.

DR. GODFREY: Hello, I'm Dr. Godfrey. And you're . . . Amy?

DAWN: Amy Sue, yes. Thank you so much for seeing me on such short notice.

DR. GODFREY: You're my last appointment of the night, so no problem at all. But what brings you in, Amy Sue? There's nothing on your intake form.

DAWN: Because I didn't want to talk to anybody but you about my situation. I rode my bike all the way from Eden as fast as I could to see you.

DR. GODFREY: Ah, you're from *Eden*. Say no more. I have great respect for the world's religions, but some of these preachers and bishops sure could use a health class or two.

DAWN: My stepdad said anybody who did the kind of work you do was an *agent of darkness*, so I kind of had to figure things out for myself. But I don't know how much I can trust him with any of this anymore, 'cause now I've got some really crazy stuff going on downstairs.

DR. GODFREY: Are you sexually active?

DAWN: No. Well. Not exactly no. But not exactly yes.

DR. GODFREY: Whatever you tell me stays in this room, Amy Sue.

DAWN: Okay but uh, my boyfriend Brock and I only did it once just a little bit, and this is going to sound absolutely crazy . . . but I think I have teeth in my vagina.

DR. GODFREY: *Teeth in your vagina?*

DAWN: I've been turning it over and over in my mind and I don't know what else to call it because Brock was in there and kinda started bleeding a little, and I just feel like maybe there's teeth growing inside me? So do you think you might be able to like . . . remove them?

DR. GODFREY: Unfortunately, I can't remove teeth from your vagina because you don't *have* teeth in your vagina, Amy Sue. I promise you. Vaginismus . . . vulvar vestibulitis, maybe. Something in the cancer neighborhood, God forbid. But teeth? Nah. But how about you change into a gown, and when you're ready we'll take a look under the hood and figure out what's going on together.

(Dawn changes behind a screen while Dr. Godfrey washes his hands.)

DAWN: So um, how *did* you get into this line of work?

GIRLS LIKE YOU

DR. GODFREY:

VAGINAS HAVE LONG ENCHANTED ME
WITH THEIR DEEP HIDDEN DEPTHS

AND THEIR LOOPS AND WHORLS
SINCE I WAS A BOY, I WAS KEEN TO SEE
JUST HOW DIFFERENT I WAS
FROM THE NEIGHBORHOOD GIRLS

DAY IN AND DAY OUT, I POKE AND PROD
WITH MY STETH AND MY SPEC
AND MY LATEX GLOVE
A CLOD AMONG MEN, AMONG VADGE I'M A GOD
EVERY RIDGE, EVERY FOLD
I EXAMINE WITH LOVE

TO KEEP IT FROM GETTING ROUTINE AND BANAL
  WITH
GIRLS. LIKE. YOU.
I JUST GO SPELUNKING IN THE BIRTH CANAL
  WITH
GIRLS. LIKE. YOU.
I'M ALWAYS SO STUNNED WHEN IT'S COY AND/
  OR SKITTISH WITH
GIRLS. LIKE. YOU.
WHEN LIPS SHOULD BE LOOSE BUT INSTEAD,
  THEY'RE SO BRITISH
WITH GIRLS LIKE YOU.

(Dawn emerges from behind the screen in a gown, giggling.)

I liked to lead with a little humor. I hope I didn't offend.

DAWN: I've been so scared that it feels good to laugh at this a little.

I KNOW I WAS RIGHT TO SEEK YOU OUT
WITH A PROBLEM LIKE THIS THAT I CAN'T
  EXPLAIN

AND WHAT COULD I HAVE THAT COULD FREAK
YOU OUT?
AS A DOCTOR, I'M SURE IT'S FAMILIAR TERRAIN

(Nervous) Right?

DR. GODFREY:

TO KEEP IT FROM GETTING BANAL AND ROUTINE
WITH
GIRLS. LIKE. YOU.
I LOOK FOR THE SECRETS DEEP IN THE VAGINE
WITH
GIRLS. LIKE. YOU.
I HATE TO SEE FEAR IN THE BEAUTIFUL EYES OF
GIRLS. LIKE. YOU.
THE TERROR YOU FEEL WITH WHAT'S BETWEEN
YOUR THIGHS
WITH GIRLS LIKE YOU.

(Dawn sits on the table.)

WELL THEN, LET'S HAVE A LOOK SINCE YOU FEEL
YOU'RE ABNORMAL
NO NEED TO TENSE UP, THIS IS ALL VERY FORMAL
I'M PROUD OF MY WORK AS A VAGINAL SCHOLAR
SO IF YOU FEEL PAIN, THEN JUST GIVE ME A
HOLLER
NOW SCOOT DOWN

(Dawn scoots.)

SCOOT DOWN

(And scoots.)

SCOOT

(And scoots.)

SCOOT

(And scoots.)

SCOOT DOWN

(And scoots.)

NOW SPREAD

(Dawn slowly spreads her legs.)

Agent of Darkness reporting for duty. Again, just a little humor. Keep me up to date with your pain scale, okay? Don't be afraid to be verbal.

(Dr. Godfrey's humor causes the Promise Keeper Girls to appear in Dawn's mind like nurses who observe at first, then eventually become more savage.)

YOU CAN'T BE TOO HASTY, YOU HAVE TO TAKE
CARE WITH
GIRLS. LIKE. YOU.

(Dr. Godfrey removes his latex gloves.)

PROMISE KEEPER GIRLS:

WE'RE COMING, WE'RE COMING, WE'RE COMING

DR. GODFREY:

YOU HAVE TO BE SUBTLE, YOU HAVE TO PREPARE WITH
GIRLS. LIKE. YOU.

(He lotions up his hands.)

PROMISE KEEPER GIRLS:

WE'RE COMING, WE'RE COMING, WE'RE COMING

DR. GODFREY:

IT'S LIKE HUNTING A DEER WHEN I HAVE TO EXAMINE
GIRLS. LIKE. YOU.

(He wags his tongue suggestively.)

PROMISE KEEPER GIRLS:

WE'RE COMING, WE'RE COMING, WE'RE COMING

DR. GODFREY:

WAIT 'TIL THE COAST IS ALL CLEAR, COUNT DOWN FROM TEN, AND BAM!

(He reaches inside her suddenly and is overwhelmed with lust.)

THIS PUSSY IS SWEET—I'VE BEEN ACHING TO EAT A
GIRL! LIKE! YOU!

(The same light we saw at the lake begins to fill the room, even stronger.)

DAWN *(Feeling discomfort)*: Ow!

PROMISE KEEPER GIRLS:

AH, AH
WE'RE COMING, WE'RE COMING, WE'RE COMING

DR. GODFREY:

I'D GIVE ALL I AM JUST TO LICK OUT THE CLAM
OF A
GIRL. LIKE. YOU.

DAWN: That isn't funny, Doctor! Ow!

PROMISE KEEPER GIRLS:

AH, AH
WE'RE COMING, WE'RE COMING, WE'RE COMING

DR. GODFREY:

I CANNOT EXPLAIN WHY I CAN'T CATCH MY
BREATH WITH
GIRLS. LIKE. YOU.

DAWN: Nine on the pain scale! Nine on the pain scale!

PROMISE KEEPER GIRLS:

AH, AH
WE'RE COMING, WE'RE COMING, WE'RE COMING

DR. GODFREY:

THE PLEASURE AND PAIN AND THEN "THE LITTLE
DEATH"

DR. GODFREY:	PROMISE KEEPER GIRLS:
WITH GIRLS LIKE	AH
GIRLS LIKE	AH
WITH GIRLS LIKE—	AH, AH—

(Dawn's body reacts and her vaginal teeth cut off his arm. A banshee cry fills the room. Dr. Godfrey's arm falls to the ground. Blood shoots everywhere.)

DR. GODFREY: It's truuuue!!! Vagina dentata! Vagina dentata! Vagina dentataaaaaaaaaaaaaaaaaaaaaaaaa!!!!!

(Dawn runs out of the room screaming, followed by PKG.)

SCENE ELEVEN

Split scene of Dawn pacing in a blood-soaked gown in Ryan's bedroom and Brad on the streets of Eden communing with Godfather.

BRAD: Is this uniform what you had in mind, Godfather?

GODFATHER: Well done, Truthseeker! Now you are ready for battle! And this is where I must leave you for the penultimate leg of your quest.

BRAD: Leave me? But what about the teeth? Where do they *come from*?

GODFATHER: To gain the answers you seek and defeat the feminocracy, you must now find the wiki within the shadows of the dark web.

BRAD: *The wiki within the shadows of the dark web?!?*

GODFATHER: The dark web is not only online. The dark web is also within. Find the wiki and all will be revealed. Let the pain in your finger be your light and lead you to the origin of the teeth.

(Brad holds up his finger, which lights up as the dark web reveals itself.)

DAWN: His hand, his hand, his hand!

RYAN *(Overlapping)*: Dawn, it's not your fault! Blame it on me! I never should have sent you to that guy!

DAWN *(Overlapping)*: And the blood! The blood! And the screaming! It was like something out of a scary movie!

RYAN: You're so tense—

DAWN: Of course, I'm tense! I'm a murderer!

RYAN: Dawn, you're not a murderer! Dr. Godfrey violated you, so I think it was justice? As a matter of fact, I'd even go as far as to say you're a superhero.

DAWN: A superhero?!?!?

RYAN: Yeah! A superhero that Father God armed with teeth so you can bite back against the patriarchy!

DAWN: But Father God IS the patriarchy!!!!

RYAN: Okay, you got me there!

DAWN: Brad told me I bit him on his finger down there when we were little. I thought he was talking crazy, but it all came flooding back to me while I was riding my bike here.

(Dawn enters a memory space.)

I wanted to know if we were the same down there. So I dared him to take his swim trunks down. And he dared me to take my swimsuit down. So I did. But when he took his down, I couldn't believe how it was hanging there like a piece of fruit. So I asked him if I could touch it, but I was scared to touch it too, so when he asked me if he could touch me first I said okay. But then he was screaming and I was screaming and there was blood in the water and Pastor started screaming at Brad and—oh God, they've been in me this whole time?!?

(The memory ends.)

RYAN: It's okay, it's okay. Wow, that's a really intense story. But it seems to me like the teeth or whatever they are only come out when something unwanted goes down there—

DAWN: But I just said that I wanted it—

RYAN: Okay, but do you remember what it feels like before they come out?

DAWN: Maybe a little pressure? I dunno! It keeps getting stronger and I feel like I'm going to black out every time it happens! Dr. Godfrey kept screaming, "Dentata!"

RYAN: "Dentata"? But that's Latin. Hmm . . . Okay. I have an idea. Go in the bathroom, take a hot bath, and clean yourself up. And while you're in there, I'm gonna do some poking around on the dark web to see if we can get to the bottom of this?

DAWN: *The dark web?* Oh God . . .

(Dawn exits. Ryan goes to his laptop and logs on to the dark web.)

ACCORDING TO THE WIKI

RYAN: Dentata. What a cool word! Den-ta-ta, den-ta-ta, den-ta-ta. *(A search result piques his interest) Ooh. Here's a wiki on myth of Dentata?* Okay. Well, let's take a look?

ACCORDING TO THE WIKI
DENTATA IS A GODDESS WHO BEATS GENESIS BY
TEN THOUSAND YEARS
ACCORDING TO THE WIKI
HER NAME JUST MEANS "TEETH"
SHE'S AT THE HEART OF MEN'S EMASCULATION
FEARS

HIDDEN IN HER LABIA
FANGS LIKE DRAC
WITH AN APPETITE FOR PENIS AS A MIDNIGHT
SNACK
THEY'RE A FEMININE PROTECTION
FROM A MASCULINE ATTACK
ACCORDING TO THE WIKI

BRAD: Truthseekers near and far! Do you feel me?!?

(The Truthseekers appear with their fingers in the air.)

TRUTHSEEKERS: We feel you, Truthseeker!

BRAD: Behold what I have learned about the leader of the feminocracy!

ACCORDING TO THE WIKI
DENTATA WAS RELENTLESS IN HER BUTCHERING
OF EVERYTHING MALE
ACCORDING TO THE WIKI
WHEREVER SHE WENT, DENTATA LEFT A GRUE-
SOME, BLOODY, PHALLIC TRAIL

TRUTHSEEKER #3:

DAWN HAS NOW EMBODIED HER WITH GREAT
SKILL

TRUTHSEEKER #1:

DENTATA REBORN
AGAINST MAN'S WILL

BRAD:

SOON SHE'LL BUILD HERSELF AN ARMY
AND ONE BY ONE, THEY'LL KILL

BRAD AND TRUTHSEEKERS:

ACCORDING TO THE WIKI

BRAD, RYAN AND TRUTHSEEKERS:

UNTIL THERE IS A HERO
A MOST UNLIKELY HERO
WHO COMES TO TOWN TO BREAK THE SPELL

BRAD:

WITH THE POWER TO DISMEMBER

RYAN:

WITH THE POWER IN HIS MEMBER

BRAD:

TO BREAK THE TEETH AND SEND THEM ON A ONE-WAY BACK TO HELL

RYAN:

AND ONLY HE OF PURITY CAN SEE THIS MISSION THROUGH

BRAD:

TO BE THAT MAN, WE HAVE TO PLAN ESSENTIALLY A COUP

BRAD, RYAN AND TRUTHSEEKERS:

AND ONLY HE OF PURITY CAN SEE THIS MISSION THROUGH
TO BE THE MAN, I HAVE TO PLAN
'CAUSE THAT'S WHAT HEROES DO

BRAD: I will defeat Dentata and her army with iron fists, brass balls, and a *cock of steel*.

Because I! AM! HEROOOOOOOOO!!!!!

(With the sound of a sword being pulled from its sheath, Brad transforms into Hero and the Truthseekers transform into Patriarchs.)

HERO AND RYAN:	PATRIARCHS:
ACCORDING TO THE WIKI	AH
THE HERO IS A MAN OF NOBLE CHARACTER AND COURAGE GALORE	
HERO:	
A PATRIARCHAL LEADER	AH
RYAN:	
THE GUY WHO RUSHES IN TO SAVE THE DAY	AH
NOT THE SODOMITE NEXT DOOR!	

HERO:

WITH THIS DICK, I'LL CONQUER HER

RYAN:

I COULD DIE

HERO:

WE WILL END THE FEMINOCRACY
OUR VIC'TRY IS NIGH

RYAN:

AND DOING THIS WILL HELP DAWN TOO
THAT'S ALWAYS BEEN THE GOAL

HERO:

SHE'S A VAGINAL BLACK HOLE
THAT'S JUST A BODY WITH NO SOUL

HERO, RYAN AND PATRIARCHS:

SHE JUST NEEDS A MAN WHO CAN BRING HER
BODY UNDER HIS CONTROL
ACCORDING TO THE WIKI!

(Hero and the Patriarchs exit. Dawn comes out of the bathroom in a robe.)

RYAN: Oh, hey there. How are you feeling? Better?

DAWN: I'm all cleaned up but honestly, I feel dirtier than ever.

RYAN: What's wrong now?

DAWN: I think I've gotta turn myself in, Ryan.

RYAN: What? No. Dawn, you can't!

DAWN: I don't have a choice! It's only a matter of time before I'm found out and—

RYAN: Or what if there's another way out of this?

DAWN: What way?

RYAN: It turns out Dentata is real.

DAWN: What?

(Ryan shows Dawn his laptop.)

RYAN: She's an ancient goddess with teeth between her legs who went on a killing spree until a hero rescued her from herself? And I don't know how or why, but I think maybe the spirit of Dentata has been using your body as a host? But I think I can help because it says in the myth that the hero of noble courage breaks the curse? Of the teeth? With his um . . . sword?

DAWN: And you think . . . *you're* "the hero"?

RYAN: Maybe? I dunno. Look, I believe in Father God with every fiber of my being. I do. But I also believe in *you*, so maybe I have to believe in this too.

DAWN: But Dentata is just a myth. There's no such thing as ancient—

RYAN: Why can't there be room for more than one God?

DAWN: Ryan, that's *idolatry*!

RYAN: Not if Dentata is a female deity that's been hidden from us for thousands of years! What if Dentata is actually like, *Mother* God? And maybe myths are only myths until enough people believe in them? What if the only way to make you whole again down there is to have faith in Dentata *too*?

(The passion of Ryan's ideological conviction stirs something in Dawn.)

DAWN: *Mother God? Dentata?* I don't know why, but hearing *you* say all this stuff makes it feel so *real*. But also, Pastor *did* say Father God told him not to go inside of my mom to heal her, but maybe he was really just afraid of *her* teeth and of being *her* hero? So if I don't let you inside of me, I could die like my mom did . . . but if I do let you inside of me and we're wrong about you being my hero, I could kill *you*!

RYAN: But even if you did kill me, I'd rather sacrifice myself trying to save you than continue to live as a homosexual abomination.

DAWN: Oh, Ryan . . . are you sure?

I'M YOUR GUY

RYAN: As sure as I'll ever be?

I'M WITH YOU HERE TONIGHT
MY HEART IS FILLED WITH FRIGHT
NEVER THOUGHT I'D END UP HERE,
ALONE WITH YOU

ON THIS NARROW LEDGE
TEETERING THE EDGE OF THE UNKNOWN

TONIGHT, IT'S PRETTY CLEAR
I MUST IGNORE MY FEAR
NO REASON I SHOULD FREEZE OR TURN TO
STONE WITH YOU
LOOK INTO MY EYES
HOPE YOU REALIZE YOU'RE NOT ALONE

I'M YOUR GUY
WHEN EVERYONE HAS LEFT YOU
I'M THE ONE
WHO IS ALWAYS STANDING BY
THROUGH THICK AND THIN
YOU CAN COUNT ME IN
YOU WILL BE PROTECTED
BECAUSE I'M YOUR GUY

SO LET'S TAKE OFF OUR CLOTHES
SHOW ME YOUR BLOOMING ROSE
I PRAY THAT I CAN BE THE MAN YOU NEED
TONIGHT
THERE'S NO TURNING BACK
HOPE I SHOW A KNACK FOR MAKING LOVE

I'M YOUR GUY
WHEN NO ONE ELSE WILL HAVE YOU
I'M THE ONE
WHO WILL NEVER MAKE YOU CRY
FROM THIS NIGHT ON
I'M HERE FOR YOU, DAWN
YOU DON'T HAVE TO WORRY
BECAUSE I'M YOUR GUY

DAWN:

BE MY GUY ALL THROUGH THE NIGHT
'TIL THE EARLY MORNING LIGHT
PROMISE YOU WILL HOLD ME TIGHT FOREVER
BE MY GUY, I WANT YOU TO
SHOW ME LOVE THAT'S PURE AND TRUE
'TIL WE'RE BORN AGAIN, BRAND NEW TOGETHER

DAWN AND RYAN:

TOGETHER

(They have extremely pleasurable, shame- and pain-free sex. Miraculously, they climax together, unharmed.)

RYAN:

I'M YOUR GUY
AND NOW THE SPELL IS BROKEN

DAWN:

YOU'RE THE ONE
MY BODY WOULDN'T LIE

DAWN AND RYAN:

DRAGONS MAY BLOW FIRE TO AND FRO
NOTHING ELSE CAN HURT ME

RYAN:

BECAUSE I'M YOUR GUY

DAWN AND RYAN:

OOH . . .

(Silence.)

DAWN: You're still all in one piece. And so am I. I'm healed. I'm healed!

RYAN: Yeah. And I'm a man now. A *real* man! Straight! I'm *straight*! I broke the curse! I don't have shame in my body anymore! And I have what it takes to please a *woman*! I mean, at least I think I do? I mean, if you don't mind my asking, how was I? You know . . . doing it?

DAWN: Honestly? You were *amazing*. And you know what? I was amazing too!

RYAN: Yeah you were!

DAWN: Sex . . . IS AMAZING! Why didn't anybody tell me?!?

RYAN *(Tickling her)*: Maybe we should get married.

DAWN *(Fending him off)*: Stop! I mean, all these years I was so scared of what it would be like because of Father God and Pastor and everything he ingrained in me about purity and PKG that I never even *imagined* sex could be like, spiritual? And part of like, a female *divinity* or whatever? My whole life in Eden feels like such a silly dream now!

RYAN: Well, it isn't *all* a dream. Tobey *is* dead. And so is Dr. Godfrey. But at least the police are one thing you don't have to worry about.

DAWN: How do you mean?

RYAN: Because I've got proof that exonerates you.

DAWN: What kind of proof?

RYAN *(Showing Dawn his computer)*: Boom.

(He presses play and we hear the sounds of them having sex moments ago.)

DAWN: What is this?

RYAN: I went live.

(Silence.)

DAWN: *You recorded us doing it?*

RYAN: Yeah.

DAWN: Everybody can see this?

RYAN: Duh. That's the point. So they can see two miracles at once.

DAWN: Miracles?

RYAN: Yeah, miracles. That I'm a real man, and that you don't have teeth down there.

DAWN: But that's . . . but . . . but you didn't *ask* me.

RYAN: If I had asked, you might've said no.

(Dawn is speechless.)

I mean, it was a little sneaky, but it's a win-win for both of us. You see that, right?

DAWN: But now everybody's gonna think I'm just some kinda whore.

RYAN: Better a whore than a murderer!

DAWN: Ryan . . .

RYAN: Look, Dawn, it's not like I ever really expected to be paid back for all the stuff I've done for you, but you do kind of owe me? So I wish you would start acting a little grateful?

(Silence.)

DAWN: Thanks.

RYAN: Absolutely. So now what? Do you want breakfast?

DAWN: Sure.

RYAN: That's right. After you fuck, you're supposed to have breakfast.

(He exits into another room. In anguish, Dawn lets out a banshee cry. The sound takes her by surprise.)

DAWN: What was that?

(The light we saw at the lake and at Dr. Godfrey's office returns and saturates Dawn, as PKG enters in a trance, transformed.

Dawn feels a sharp cramp. She subsequently begins to moan and groan and violently thrash on the bed. A spirit begins to overtake her from the inside.)

WHEN SHE GAVE BIRTH (REPRISE)

KEKE:

THEN WE GAVE BIRTH TO KILLING RAGE

KEKE AND BECKY:

AND WHAT WAS LEFT OF OUR SOULS FELL AWAY

KEKE, BECKY AND STEPHANIE:

'TWAS MASCULINE SUPREMACY THAT SET THE STAGE

KEKE, BECKY, STEPHANIE AND TRISHA:

FOR MAN'S DEFEAT AND JUDGMENT DAY

KEKE, BECKY, STEPHANIE, TRISHA AND RACHAEL:

FOR MAN'S DEFEAT AND JUDGMENT DAY

KEKE, BECKY, STEPHANIE, TRISHA, RACHAEL AND FIONA:

THE TIME HAS COME TO MAKE THEM OUR PREY
TO HUNT THEM DOWN
AND MAKE THEM ALL PAY!!!!!

(Dawn's vaginal teeth reemerge and the spirit completes its possession of her body. We are now with the goddess Dentata.)

DENTATA

DENTATA:

AND SO I RISE—I HAVE HEARD YOUR PRAYER
I'M BETWEEN YOUR THIGHS—I AM EVERYWHERE

PROMISE KEEPER GIRLS:

DENTATA DENTATA DENTATA
DENTATA DENTATA DENTATA

DENTATA:

INSIDE I BURN LIKE A FIRE DOES
'CAUSE I'VE RID THIS FLESH OF THE GIRL IT WAS

PROMISE KEEPER GIRLS:

DENTATA DENTATA DENTATA
DENTATA DENTATA DENTATA

DENTATA:

I TREMBLE SOME, BUT I HAVE NO FEAR
THEN I JUST GO NUMB
'CAUSE THE CHOICE IS CLEAR

PROMISE KEEPER GIRLS:

DENTATA DENTATA DENTATA DENTATA

(Dentata positions herself on the bed. Ryan reenters with a breakfast tray.)

RYAN: Breakfast!
DENTATA: Actually, I'm hungry. But not for that.
RYAN: But it's Grape-Nuts.
DENTATA: I don't want Grape-Nuts. I want *your* nuts.

RYAN: Really? You wanna do it again?
DENTATA: It's all I can think about.
RYAN: Okay! Well let's go, little lady.

(He puts down the breakfast tray and goes to her.)

DENTATA:

THE MOON TURNS RED AND THE LINES ALL BLUR
AND THOUGH I'M RIGHT HERE
ALL HE SEES IS HER

PROMISE KEEPER GIRLS:

DENTATA DENTATA DENTATA

DENTATA: Stick it in me, big boy.
RYAN: I can't believe that used to be my line.

DENTATA:

I'M A HAZY SHAPE THAT HE CAN'T QUITE TRACK
WITH A BLOODY CAPE FLOWING DOWN MY BACK

PROMISE KEEPER GIRLS:

DENTATA DENTATA DENTATA

RYAN: Wait. Wait. Dawn? What's going on? Something doesn't feel right.

DENTATA:

I WEAR DAWN'S FACE, BUT IT'S JUST A MASK
AT A GLACIAL PACE I BEGIN MY TASK

(Dentata bites Ryan with her vaginal teeth. She pulls his penis from between her legs and dangles it in front of his face. He makes a grab for it, but she yanks it out of reach and pockets it.)

PROMISE KEEPER GIRLS:

DENTATA DENTATA DENTATA DENTATA DENTATA

RYAN *(Screams)*: AHHHHHHHHHHHHHHHHHH!!!!!!!!

PROMISE KEEPER GIRLS:

TRUST NO MAN
FEAR NO MAN
SNAKES IN HER GARDEN

DENTATA:

DENTATA DENTATA DENTATA DENTATA DENTATA

PROMISE KEEPER GIRLS:

TRUST NO MAN
FEAR NO MAN
SNAKES IN HER GARDEN

Who's next, Goddess?

DENTATA: The Pastor.

PROMISE KEEPER GIRLS: The Pastor! *(Rhythmically repeating, overlapping with Dentata)* The Pastor! The Pastor! The Pastor! The Pastor!

DENTATA: We must *crush* the oppressor and his purity and his fig leaves and his Father God! He must pay!

(The girls hiss as Dentata exits. They then proceed to dispose of Ryan's body.)

PROMISE KEEPER GIRLS *(Slinking into the shadows)*:

NO MORE VIRGIN PROMISES TO KEEP
NO MORE BEING ONE OF PASTOR'S SHEEP
WE DESERVE OUR PIECE OF SHEPHERD'S PIE
QUICKLY THOUGH, THE TIME IS DRAWING NIGH

(Pastor enters the NTV sanctuary dressed for battle in the unholy war. He carries a large dagger.)

PASTOR: Show yourselves, succubi! Step into the light!

(The Promise Keeper Girls reveal themselves to Pastor, who gets progressively more afraid.)

PROMISE KEEPER GIRLS *(An ominous greeting)*: PASTOR.
PASTOR: The time of reckoning is at hand!
PROMISE KEEPER GIRLS: IT IS!
PASTOR: You have allowed the beast to penetrate you.
PROMISE KEEPER GIRLS: WE HAVE.
PASTOR: So I must seal your vaginal lips shut and send you to Hell forever!
PROMISE KEEPER GIRLS: HELL IS HERE.

(They hiss.)

PASTOR: Your dark magics may engorge my manhood, but Father God's vengeance is mighty!
STEPHANIE: OUR VAGINAL LIPS SPEAK TO A HIGHER POWER THAN *YOURS*, PASTOR.
PASTOR: The Power of Christ compels you to *release* me, you she-whore!!!

(Dentata appears in her ceremonial dress.)

DENTATA: AND THE POWER OF *DENTATA* COMPELS YOU TO SHUT THE FUCK UP AND GIVE US YOUR BIG FAT *DICK*!

(PKG falls on him like the Bacchae, ripping off his clothes. Eventually, they rape him and vaginally cut off his penis.)

MY GIFT HAS SPREAD LIKE A PLAGUE WORLDWIDE
SOON, ALL MEN WILL FALL TO OUR GENOCIDE

PROMISE KEEPER GIRLS:
DENTATA DENTATA DENTATA DENTATA DENTATA

PASTOR: AHHHHHHHHHHHHHHHHHHHHH!!!!!!!!

PROMISE KEEPER GIRLS:
TRUST NO MAN
FEAR NO MAN
SNAKES IN HER GARDEN

DENTATA:
DENTATA DENTATA DENTATA DENTATA DENTATA

PROMISE KEEPER GIRLS:
TRUST NO MAN
FEAR NO MAN
SNAKES IN HER GARDEN

(Dentata sniffs the air.)

DENTATA: Mmm! What's that smell, sisters?
PROMISE KEEPER GIRLS: SAUSAGE PARTY!!!!

(Dentata and PKG exit. Hero enters the NTV sanctuary with a quiet but noticeable swagger. He sees Pastor on the floor, bleeding and disabled.)

PASTOR: The pain . . . I'm finally free of the pain and the shame of my precious gift . . . I'm finally free of the meat of Adam . . .

(Hero begins to pour lighter fluid on Pastor as though he's pissing on him.)

HERO: Pathetic. Only a *cuck* would glory in his own body's emasculation.

PASTOR: Son . . . it's so much better this way . . .

HERO: Your son is *dead*. I killed him. There is only Hero now.

PASTOR: She set me free, she made me clean . . . she can make you clean too . . .

HERO: Your duty was to domesticate the body of Woman, and you failed—first with your first wife, Lilith, and then with your second wife, Kim, which allowed Dentata to take root in the virgin bodies of your stepdaughter and her PKG coven. Your failure is a betrayal.

PASTOR *(Overlapping)*: *"For God so loved the world that He gave His only begotten son, that whosoever shall believe in Him shall not perish but have everlasting life—"*

HERO: Oh, *shut up*. Because the only one who's going to perish is you, *cuck*.

(Hero stuffs the dismembered penis in Pastor's mouth.)

So ungird your loins. Eat the fruit.

(Hero lights the match, mocking him.)

And hands up for Father God!

(He drops it on Pastor, then runs out to watch New Testament Village burn. PKG reenters, chanting.)

PROMISE KEEPER GIRLS:

SHE WILL SEE YOU VERY SOON, YOU DUMMY

HERO: Burn.

PROMISE KEEPER GIRLS:
SHE WILL SEE YOU VERY SOON, YOU FOOL

HERO: *Burn!*

PROMISE KEEPER GIRLS:
GONNA GET YOU WITH HER POON, YOU DUMMY

HERO: *Burn*, fucker!

(Hero begins to laugh.)

PROMISE KEEPER GIRLS:
GONNA GET YOU WITH HER POON, YOU FOOL
SHE'LL SEE YOU VERY SOON, YOU DUMMY

HERO:
I FEEL HER UNDERNEATH MY SKIN

PROMISE KEEPER GIRLS:
SHE'LL SEE YOU VERY SOON, YOU FOOL

HERO:
SHE'S THERE BEHIND MY EYES

PROMISE KEEPER GIRLS:
GONNA GET YOU WITH HER POON, YOU DUMMY

HERO:
BUT WHEN WE LOCK HORNS, FINALLY

PROMISE KEEPER GIRLS:
GONNA GET YOU WITH HER POON, YOU FOOL

HERO:

SHE'S IN FOR A SURPRISE!

Come to me, Patriarchs!

(Patriarchs #1 and #2 enter.)

PATRIARCHS #1 AND #2: Yes, Hero!

HERO: Sniff the air and let the foul stench of feminocratic pussy guide you to your target. Use your cocks of steel to heal them of their teeth, but leave Dentata to me! Stop the fall of mankind!

PATRIARCHS #1 AND #2: Stop the fall of mankind!

(Hero exits, and Patriarchs #1 and #2 fan out. Patriarch #1 spots a Promise Keeper Girl and tries to defang her.)

PATRIARCH #1: This dick is to dismantle the feminocratic—

(Patriarch #1 adlibs fear and surprise as the girls quickly disable him and, letting out a banshee cry, proceed to rape him.)

PROMISE KEEPER GIRLS: CHOP! CHOP!

PATRIARCH #1 *(Screams)*: AHHHHHHHHHH!!!!!!!!

(Patriarch #2 goes to defang another member of PKG.)

PATRIARCH #2: This dick is for patriarchs and heroes who—

(Patriarch #2 adlibs fear and surprise as the girls quickly disable him and, letting out a banshee cry, rape him as well.)

PROMISE KEEPER GIRLS: CHOP! CHOP!

PATRIARCH #2 *(Screams)*: AHHHHHHHHHH!!!!!!!!

(We then see Patriarch #3 getting a lethal blowjob from Promise Keeper Girl Becky.)

PATRIARCH #3: This cock is made of steel!

(All of PKG except Becky lets out a banshee cry.)

This cock will make you squeal!

(All of PKG except Becky lets out a banshee cry.)

This cock will make you heal!

(Dentata steps out of the shadows and calls out to Patriarch #3.)

DENTATA: That cock will be my meal!
PATRIARCH #3: Huh?
DENTATA AND PROMISE KEEPER GIRLS: CHOP! CHOP!
PATRIARCH #3 *(Screams)*: AHHHHHHHHHH!!!!!!!!

DENTATA:
I KILL THEM ALL
AND I HAVE NO SHAME
AS THEIR BODIES FALL
THEY CRY OUT MY NAME

PROMISE KEEPER GIRLS:
DENTATA DENTATA DENTATA DENTATA DENTATA

SPREAD YOUR WINGS
SPREAD YOUR LEGS
SNAKES IN YOUR GARDEN
DENTATA DENTATA DENTATA
DENTATA DENTATA DENTATA

DENTATA:

SPREAD MY WINGS

SPREAD MY LEGS

SNAKES IN MY GARDEN

SNAKES IN MY GARDEN

SNAKES IN MY GARDEN

SNAKES IN MY GARDEN

PROMISE KEEPER GIRLS:

DENTATA

DENTATA

DENTATA

DENTATA

DENTATA

DENTATA AND PROMISE KEEPER GIRLS:

DENTATA DENTATA DENTATA!
DENTATA!

(Dentata and PKG stand triumphant amongst the emasculated Patriarchs. Dentata surveys the destruction that lies in her wake with great pleasure. After a moment, she sniffs the air.)

DENTATA: You can come out from hiding now, Hero! I won't bite! *Not yet, anyway.*

(Hero enters.)

HERO: Your teeth are no match for my manhood, you feminocratic cunt.

DENTATA *(Laughing at him)*: Is that so? Well, how's *your finger* feeling, Hero?

HERO: Shut your fucking mouth! Let's end this!

DENTATA: With pleasure!

(PKG begins a chant, joined by the undead Patriarchs.)

TAKE ME DOWN

PROMISE KEEPER GIRLS AND PATRIARCHS *(Chanting on a loop)*:

SEX
BODIES
PAIN
SHAME
GUILT
WATER
FIRE
DEATH

(Dentata steps forward to face Hero. They eventually battle.)

HERO:

YOU ARE THE MONSTER

DENTATA:

YOU ARE THE MONSTER

HERO:

THAT MUST BE SLAIN

DENTATA:

THAT MUST BE SLAIN

HERO AND DENTATA:

YOU ARE THE ORIGIN, ORIGIN, ORIGIN OF MY PAIN

DENTATA:

YOU ARE THE MONSTER

HERO:

YOU ARE THE MONSTER

DENTATA:

THAT'S IN MY BRAIN

HERO:

THAT'S IN MY BRAIN

HERO AND DENTATA:

AND I'LL DIE BEFORE I LET YOU TAKE ME DOWN

DENTATA:

I AM YOUR MONSTER

HERO:

I AM YOUR MONSTER

DENTATA:

CLOAKED IN THE NIGHT

HERO:

CLOAKED IN THE NIGHT

HERO AND DENTATA:

YOU CONJURE ME, CONJURE ME, CONJURE ME
TO SATE YOUR MYTHIC APPETITE

DENTATA:

I AM THE MONSTER

HERO:

I AM THE MONSTER

DENTATA:

THAT YOU MUST FIGHT

HERO:

THAT YOU MUST FIGHT

HERO AND DENTATA:

AND I'LL DIE BEFORE I LET YOU TAKE ME DOWN

I'M HERE
I'M HERE
TAKE OFF YOUR CLOTHES
LET ME TASTE YOUR FEAR
YOUR FEAR
LET ME SEE YOUR MONSTER!
YOUR MONSTER!!
YOUR MONSTER! YOUR MONSTER! YOUR
MONSTER!
SO I CAN TAKE YOU DOWN! DOWN! DOWN!
TAKE YOU DOWN! DOWN! DOWN!
TAKE YOU DOWN! DOWN! DOWN!
TAKE YOU DOWN!

(Blackout.)

SCENE TWELVE

Lights up on the fallout of the war between Hero and Dentata. It's gloomy and dark, save for intermittent lighting. Silence except for intermittent thunder.

Hero lies dead on the ground, emasculated. The Patriarchs are now zombie Cucks. The Promise Keeper Girls are now Feminocrats of Dentata, who stands holding Hero's severed penis by her side. Her mouth is smeared with blood, as if she's just eaten flesh. She smiles. She drops the penis to the ground like it's nothing.

FEMINOCRATS: Who's next, Goddess?
DENTATA *(Testing them)*: Who do you think?
FEMINOCRAT FIONA: The holdouts.
FEMINOCRAT BECKY: The nonbelievers.
FEMINOCRAT RACHAEL: The *infidels*.
FEMINOCRAT KEKE: For unto them a savior is born!

(The Feminocrats let out a banshee cry.)

FEMINOCRAT TRISHA: With the awesome power of the *feminocracy* in her hand!

(The Feminocrats let out a banshee cry.)

FEMINOCRAT BECKY: In Dentata's feminocracy, *no one* is free until *everyone* is free!!!

DENTATA *(Another test)*: And *who* are the freedom fighters? *Who* are the liberators?!?

FEMINOCRATS: We are! We are!

DENTATA: And who made Dentata's rebirth necessary?

FEMINOCRAT TRISHA: The Ryans.

FEMINOCRAT RACHAEL: The Godfreys.

FEMINOCRAT KEKE: The Tobeys.

FEMINOCRAT FIONA: The Pastors.

FEMINOCRAT BECKY: Even the Adams.

FEMINOCRAT STEPHANIE: The *heroes*.

DENTATA: All mankind. For it was *they* who forced your legs open or shut. It was *they* whose fear and mistrust sharpened your teeth. Now it is they who are *cucks* for the feminocracy.

FEMINOCRAT BECKY: And what of the women who still oppose you, Goddess?

DENTATA: Those ungrateful cunts will face the *worst* of my wrath! Because in *this* republic, we hunt and murder *all* our ideological enemies. In the republic of Dentata, you're either *with us*—

CUCKS AND FEMINOCRATS: Or *against us*!

DENTATA: Precisely. Cucks! Feminocrats! At attention!

(The Cucks and Feminocrats obey her command. Dentata notices a dead Cuck on the ground.)

Wake up, Brad! Do you think the feminocracy and the rise of Woman has nothing to do with *you*?!?!?

(Brad the Cuck comes to life in an emasculated zombie state.)

BRAD THE CUCK: Yes, Goddess. I'm sorry, Goddess. Whatever you say, Goddess.
DENTATA: Good dog.

(Brad joins the Cucks. A Feminocrat picks up an apple.)

FEMINOCRAT KEKE: What about the apple, Goddess?
DENTATA: To Hell with that accursed thing! Father God is *dead*! And where Eve was weak, we are strong, which means we most certainly won't fall for the fruit of man again. *Smash it.*

(Keke smashes the apple underfoot. Dentata and her horde assemble.)

Onward!
CUCKS AND FEMINOCRATS: Onward!

(The army begins to march toward us, their prey.)

DENTATA:
WE ARE THE MONSTER
YOU CAN'T EXPLAIN
WE ARE THE ORIGIN, ORIGIN, ORIGIN
OF NEW PAIN
WE ARE THE MONSTER
THAT CAN'T BE SLAIN
AND WE WANT

(It begins to rain.)

ALL:

FEAR, POWER, PAIN, DEATH!
FEAR, POWER, PAIN, DEATH!
FEAR, POWER, PAIN, DEATH!
FEAR, POWER, PAIN, DEATH!
FEAR, POWER, PAIN, DEATH!
FEAR, POWER, PAIN, DEATH!!
FEAR, POWER, PAIN, DEATH!!!
FEAR, POWER, PAIN, DEATH!!!!

CUCKS AND FEMINOCRATS:

BEWARE WHAT LIES BENEATH!
OUR LOINS ARE BOTH A SWORD AND SHEATH!
YOU'LL PRAY FOR A FUN'RAL WREATH AS WE
FEAST ON YOUR FLESH AND LICK OUR TEETH!

(Dentata vibrates powerfully in the light of universal domination.

Blackout.)

END OF PLAY

BEOWULF SHEEHAN

MICHAEL R. JACKSON was one of *TIME* magazine's 100 most influential people of 2022. His Pulitzer Prize– and New York Drama Critics' Circle–winning *A Strange Loop* (which had its 2019 world premiere at Playwrights Horizons, in association with Page 73 Productions) received eleven Tony nominations in 2022, and was called "a full-on laparoscopy of the heart, soul, and loins," as well as a "gutsy, jubilantly anguished musical with infectious melodies" by Ben Brantley for the *New York Times*. In addition to *A Strange Loop*, he also wrote the book, music, and lyrics for *White Girl in Danger*, and the book and lyrics for *Teeth*, which opened at New World Stages in the fall of 2024. Awards and associations include: a New Professional Theatre Festival Award, a Jonathan Larson Grant, a Lincoln Center Emerging Artist Award, an ASCAP Foundation Harold Adamson Lyric Award, a Whiting Award, the Helen Merrill Award for Playwriting, an Outer Critics Circle Award, a Drama Desk Award, an Obie Award, a Fred Ebb Award, a Windham-Campbell Prize, a Dramatist Guild Fellowship, and he is an alum of Page 73's Interstate 73 Writers Group.

LUKE REDMOND

ANNA K. JACOBS is a Jonathan Larson Grant– and Billie Burke Ziegfeld Award–winning composer, lyricist, and book writer. In collaboration with Michael R. Jackson, she wrote the music and co-wrote the book for the Drama Desk Award– and Lucille Lortel–nominated musical *Teeth*, which *Vulture* hailed as a "bloody, bawdy musical with banging songs." It ran Off-Broadway at Playwrights Horizons and New World Stages, and an original cast recording has been released with Yellow Sound Label. Anna's stage adaptation of *Moana* is in residence at the Walt Disney Theatre onboard the *Disney Treasure*. Her other musicals include *POP!* (Yale Rep, City Theatre in Pittsburgh, Studio Theatre in Washington, DC; CT Critics Circle Award, Best Production of a Musical); *Anytown* (George Street Playhouse); *Harmony, Kansas* (Diversionary Theatre; Craig Noel Award nomination, Outstanding New Musical and Outstanding New Score); and *Witnesses* (California Center for the Arts; Craig Noel Award, Outstanding New Musical). In collaboration with playwright Anna Ziegler, she is also writing *A House Without Windows*, a musical about the life and disappearance of child prodigy author Barbara Newhall Follett. Anna received her MFA in Musical Theatre Writing from NYU-Tisch and has taught musical theater writing to students at Princeton, The New School, the New York Youth Symphony, and for the Johnny Mercer Foundation. Originally from Sydney, Australia, she has called Brooklyn home since 2006. www.annakjacobs.com